PAṬICCASAMUPPĀDA (Dependent Origination)

Part 2

Achieving Transcendence

by

Ron Wijewantha

Buddhist Publication Society
Kandy • Sri Lanka

Buddhist Publication Society
P.O. Box 61
54, Sangharaga Mawatha
Kandy - Sri Lanka

National Library of Sri Lanka -
Cataloguing-in-Publication Data

Wijewantha, Ron
Paṭiccasamuppāda (Dependent Origination): Achieving Transcendence/
R. Wijewantha; - Kandy : Buddhist Publication Society,
2003 - 126pp.; 17.5cm. (Wheel)

ISBN 955-24-0258-1
i. 294.34435 DDC 21 ii. title

1. Meditation (Buddhism) 2 Buddhism

Printed in Sri Lanka by
Quality Printers (Pvt) Ltd.
17/2, Pangiriwatta Road,
Gangodawila, Nugegoda
011- 4-302312

The Wheel Publication No. 455/457

Table of Contents

(Continued from Wheel 450-452)

To

Sita

Acknowledgements

I am indeed grateful to the Buddhist Publication Society for issuing this current tract as a Wheel Publication, so that the same readers as the first, as well as a new audience, can have access to these essays. Hopefully, we may see the day when both unabridged parts are integrated and reprinted as a single volume.

My thanks to Professors Lily de Silva and Chitra Wickramasuriya, my mentor Ven. M. Seelawimala Maha Thera, and kalyana mittas Martha Craft and Sondra Jewell who took the time to read through these essays and offer constructive criticism. I am also thankful to Ven. T. Shantarakshita Maha Thera and Ven. H. Medhananda for helping me with relavent Pali sutta passages and Sinhala commentaries thereon.

I have quoted rather copiously from many authors, and I wish to acknowledge and offer my grateful thanks to them and their respective publishers, too numerous to be mentioned individually.

Thanks also to my daughters Kamini, Chinta and Niromi for much help and encouragement, and my grandsons Ashok, Avinda and Arjun for computer assistance. My brother Emil and my brother-in-law cum best friend Wickrama Atukorale helped me in many tangible and intangible ways. My sincere thanks to them.

Mr A.G.S. Kariyawasam has once again helped with the editing of this book with his usual elegant style. My thanks to him.

It is with much pleasure that I dedicate this writing to my dearest wife Sita, who has shared with me the joys and sorrows and the vicissitudes of life for almost half a century, making me, I hope, a better person each passing day.

May all of the above persons share in the merit arising from this presentation, for the gift of the Dhamma surpasses all other gifts.

I shall feel amply rewarded if I have assisted at least a few of my readers in some little way, particularly advanced *vipassanā* meditators in Sri Lanka, Asia and in the West, by guiding them in the right direction. Hopefully, they will feel encouraged to think freely and adopt a scientific approach while maintaining the integrity of the Buddha-word as another way of pressing forward on their journey to transcend the mundane and achieve the supra-mundane, thereby joining the ranks of the Ariyas - the Noble Ones.

May our journey through saṃsāra be short and free of difficulties.

Ron W.
June 2003

Author's Preface

This presentation is essentially a continuation of the discussions on *Paṭiccasamuppāda* in *The Road to Liberation* (Wheel 450-452). Many readers considered it incomplete without specific instructions on how to arrive a step closer to liberation. They also wanted more information on the interconnectedness and inter-relationships of *Paṭiccasamuppāda* to the Four Noble Truths and the Four Foundations of Mindfulness, and how a study of the three together could make our understanding easier. But, most importantly, there was a demand for a list of the minimum amount of doctrinal texts and simple *vipassanā* meditation instructions that could lead a dedicated person to transcendence.

I hope this current presentation will fill this vacuum. For I believe that the achievement of awakening is made easier when we engage the original doctrine of *Paṭiccasamuppāda* and the original teaching of the Four Noble Truths together with *Satipaṭṭhāna* in our understanding of the fundamentals of the Dhamma. *Vipassanā* meditation practice only comes thereafter. Our experience shows that Western readers in particular benefit most when this method is adopted. My mentor, Ven. Seelawimala Mahathera, has quite correctly pointed out to me that in regard to explaining the essence of the Buddha Dhamma, erudite and knowledgeable members of the Sangha can play a very important part. The Buddha said that one should make the Dhamma one's island and refuge. It is therefore preferable for the earnest meditator to first acquaint himself wherever possible with this Dhamma base before proceeding to find a *vipassanā* meditation master. This will undoubtedly make the latter's guidance much easier to follow.

I have also added the relevant sections of the Bāhiya, the Anāthapiṇḍika, the Rāhulovāda, as well as the Anattalakkhaṇa Suttas, because of their importance in meditating on *anicca, dukkha* and *anatta.* I can personally vouch for the fact that repeated reading and contemplation on these suttas during one's own meditation sessions can result in insights, bringing a person closer to, or even to, transcendence, when the conditions are just right.

I would also like to explain the reasons for the inclusion of the experiences of an experinced *vipassanā* meditator whose approach towards transcendence would appear superficially to be quite different to that which had been adopted by the traditionalists. His experiences show that there are "many possible paths which lead to the top of a mountain". Any of the paths could surely be adopted provided that they are in accordance with the Dhamma. Our senior *vipassanā* meditator had used his knowledge of *Paṭiccasamuppāda*, the Four Noble Truths and the Satipaṭṭhānas to meditate deeply (with *sati-sampajañña*) to reach transcendence. His seeing the Dhamma from a modern perspective and the use of more recent scientific information only helped him to comprehend and gain insight into the Dhamma much faster. But transcendence was possible only when he finally focused on the three characteristics of human existence, namely *anicca*, *dukkha* and anatta – impermanence, distress and the absence of a continuing and permanent 'I.'

There may be some readers who may perhaps conclude from reading this book that I have been overly critical of present day *vipassanā* teachers. To the contrary, I have the deepest respect for these dedicated teachers. My submissions are only to the effect that it is vitally important that these teachers should impart to their pupils the core substance or essence contained in a number of other important suttas in addition to the Mahāsatipaṭṭhāna Sutta, and the Four Noble Truths. For they would know from their own experiences that it was only when they meditated with a broader perspective and understanding of the Buddha's teachings, that they comprehended and understood the truth of *anicca*, *dukkha* and *anatta* and thereby reached the threshold of liberation, or in fact, the first stage of liberation.

Ron W.
June 2003

Sutta Sources

Abreviations:

D : Dīgha Nikāya
M : Majjhima Nikāya
A : Anguttara Nikāya
Ud : Udāna
Dhp : Dhammapada
Vis : Visudhimagga

Thef text lists the sutras by their Pali name followed by the canonical reference, as shown below.

- Dīgha and Majjhima Nikāya: sutta no. e.g., D.16.
- Saṃyutta Nikāya: saṃyutta name and sutta no. e.g., Devata Saṃy. 12 refers to the 12th sutta in the Devata Saṃyutta.
- Anguttara Nikāya: nipāta and sutta, e.g., IV 23 refers to the 23rd sutta in the Book of the Fours.
- Udāna: vagga (chapter) and sutta.
- Dhammapada: gatha (verse) no.
- Visudhimagga: chapter no.

Namo tassa bhagavato arahato sammāsambudhassa

(Homage to Him, the Exalted, the Worthy, the Fully Enlightened One!)

CHAPTER VIII

Preliminary

Many of us meditators have been practising *vipassanā* meditation for decades, but have found that although we were able to reach a high level of serenity (*samatha*), we could not make a breakthrough to a supramundane state. We have often asked ourselves why there aren't more known cases of living *Ariyas*,[1] and why we have failed to become enlightened in spite of following the meditation teachers conscientiously.

The follow-up questions arising therefrom would be: "Are we as meditators at fault or do we lack the *pāramitās*[2] for liberation in this life, or, on the contrary, are the meditation methodologies of these various schools of *vipassanā* practice deficient in some aspect or another?"

Whenever these doubts are raised, teachers would often say that they are merely instructors and that we have to do the work ourselves. If we look at these teachers objectively, can we truly say that they are all 'on-the-path'? If they are not, then will it not be correct to assume that what they teach is suspect? It seems to me that if a teacher at the outset says, "I too happen to be a mere practitioner, but perhaps more experienced than you. So if you follow my instructions I shall guide you along the *vipassanā* highway, and I shall tell you when I come to areas which I have not explored before." I, for one, would respect such frankness and would be willing to practise with such a person till it was time to either find a more qualified teacher, or I felt competent to proceed on my own.

True enough, there were well-documented cases during the lifetime of the Buddha of persons like Ven. Poṭhila who had learnt the Dhamma under the Buddha, and had guided a large number of pupils to become *Ariyas*, although he was not one of them himself. It was only when the Buddha reprimanded him that he saw the light, got himself enrolled under one of his erst-while pupils and attained to the supramundane state. (*Dhp.* 282)

We now live 2550 years later, and it is extremely difficult to assess whether our *vipassanā* teachers are in fact really enlight-ened or on the way to enlightenment, or whether they are unwit-ting instruments of "the blind leading the blind". We have heard of genuine meditation masters such as Ven.Mahasi Sayadaw, Ven. Achan Chah, Upasika Kee Nanayon, Ven. Ananda Maitriya, Ven. Sri Nanarama, Ven. Henepola Gunaratana, Ven. U. Silananda, Ven. U Pandita, S.N.Goenka, Joseph Goldstein and Jack Kornfield to name a few. But of the other thousands of current teachers, only a very few appear to be qualified in the sense that while they may personally know the Dhamma more than adequately, they perhaps may not be imparting the totality of their doctrinal knowledge to their respective students.

This means that it is necessary that we follow the instructions of these second and third generation latter-day teachers with reservation. For, it may become necessary to fortify ourselves with additional Dhamma information and better meditation methodology, including the selection of more appropriate meditation subjects, dependent on our individual needs and aptitudes, before we can advance to finality. Thus, it is a fact that even the five ascetics could not become arahants simply by listening to the Buddha's first sermon, the Dhammacakkappavattana Sutta (Sacca Saṃy. 11).

It is said that the Buddha had to teach them over a period of time before he felt that they were sufficiently versed in the Dhamma, and in proper *vipassanā* meditation techniques and were then able to comprehend what he had to say. It was then that he preached the Anattalakkhaṇa Sutta* (Kanda Samy.59) [3]. The Buddhist scriptures tell us that it was on listening to this sermon that all five of them reached arahantship. There are also a number of cases where the Buddha himself had observed that the subjects for meditation adopted by certain meditators were inappropriate. By giving them alternative subjects, he had ensured their success. (*Dhp.* 25 and 285). But in these cases it would not be incorrect to assume that these meditators already had a comprehensive understanding of the essentials of the Buddha *Dhamma*.

---

* This sutta appears in the Khanda Saṃyutta as the Pañcavaggiya Sutta, but is now popularly known as the Anattalakkhaṇa Sutta.

The Buddha's final advice to Ananda just before his *Parinibbāna* was as follows:

> "Therefore Ananda, be islands unto yourselves, refuges unto yourselves, seeking no external refuge, with the *Dhamma* as your island, the *Dhamma* as your refuge, seeking no other refuge..." (Mahā Parinibbāna Sutta [D.16]).

Let us therefore keep this in mind when we listen to *vipassanā* meditation instructors.

As a further safeguard, when selecting a teacher we should ask ourselves the following questions:

1. What do previous students say of the teacher?
2. Is he well versed in the *Dhamma*?
3. Are his teachings in accord with the *Dhamma*?
4. Does the teacher show compassion and is he/she a good role model?
5. Are the Paṭiccasamupāda, the Four Noble Truths and the Mahā Satipaṭṭhāna Sutta (D.22), all used in his/her instructions?

There are many books on *vipassanā* meditation. Most of them are very useful. A list of some of the important texts was provided in Wheel publication 450-452, along with brief instructions on how a person can arrive at the threshold of the supramundane path by following a well-planned course in *vipassanā* meditation.

There are, however, a number of readers who, in spite of intensive application, have so far failed to progress. Such meditators should first take the time to stop and look inwards and ask themselves whether in reality they are beyond reproach in regard to their morality and whether they have cultivated an ability to concentrate and be mindful at all times. In other words, whether in fact they are following strictly the Noble Eightfold Path of morality-concentration-wisdom (*sīla-samādhi-paññā).*

If they are lacking in morality, this is the time to fix the problem. Morality is indeed the root system that nourishes the tree of knowledge, the tree whose trunk is 'concentration' and 'mindfulness', and whose crown is *samatha* and *vipassanā* meditation. Meditators must also further develop the four sublime states of universal loving-kindness, compassion, sympathetic joy and equanimity, and, in fact, become living monuments to these states if they are to succeed in achieving transcendence.

CHAPTER IX

Experiences of an Experinced Meditator

Before describing the methods of applied meditation, we could perhaps benefit more by first reading about the real life experiences of an experinced *vipassanā* meditator who discusses his personal voyage of discovery on the assurance of anonymity. In this account he traces his life's journey starting as a novice in meditation to the point of transcendence:

"I commenced *samatha* and *vipassanā* meditation in a rather experimental manner for a number of decades, but with little success. Since then, I have been exposed to the meditation techniques of a number of meditation masters. I have also often reread selected tracts of the *Dhamma* relating to Awakening until I found for myself a technique of *vipassanā* meditation where the ultimate focus was on a full understanding of *Paṭiccasamuppāda,* the Four Noble Truths, the Four Foundations of Mindfulness (*Satipaṭṭhāna)* and the comprehension of their interrelationship.

"My meditation culminated eventually, without conscious effort, in an automatic paradigm shift which focused on the three universal characteristics of the human condition, namely: *anicca, dukkha* and *anatta:* impermanence, distress and non-ego or 'non-I'. This method has as its foundation the strict practice of morality in all daily activities, and the cultivation of the *Brahma-vihāras* of loving-kindness, compassion, non-envious joy and equanimity.

"At this point I realized experientially that, without practising morality and mindfulness at every moment of one's waking hour, genuine progress was impossible. As a *vipassanā* meditator, it now became possible, with proper application for me even to experience briefly the *jhānas* [1]. For one can say that at such a time one is established in mindfulness and pinpointed focus on the subject of his choice. This is compatible with the *Paṭisambhidāmagga* where it is stated that as an insight meditator directs his mind to a particular section of formations, he goes on reflecting with perseverance, and his concentration will gather the same degree of strength as absorption concentration. Also, as the meditator equipped with this kind of concentration continues to reflect on the formations, insight knowledge will develop and this consciousness comes to be reckoned as a *jhāna* in itself.

"Now, without making the same mistake as the monk Sāti, [2] I can picture myself travelling in *saṃsāra* as an ever-changing stream of conditioned consciousness. It is in the form of an infinitesimally tiny bundle of ever-changing particles of energy subject to conditionality and containing within itself the totality of the *saṃsāric kammic* energy and life's experiences. In the Āneñjasappāya Sutta (M.106) this is called *samvattanikaṃ viññāṇaṃ* or the consciousness that links on. However, this does not imply that this consciousness remains unchanged and in the same state throughout the cycle of existence. Now, when I find myself in pinpointed focus on the twelve links of *Paṭiccasamuppāda* (dependent origination) in the forward direction (*anu-*

loma), I realize that the way to unbind or unravel this bundle has to be effected by dissipating its energy.

"An example of this conditioned stream of consciousness is seen in the descriptions given by the Buddha in the Jataka stories, of how he fared in *saṃsāra* in previous existences. His stream of conditioned consciousness having taken 'residence' in different bodies, or *nāma-rūpas,* in accordance with the immanent law of *kamma,* would exist in this fashion until it was time for this ever-changing energy to move on to the next rebirth.

"I now realize that this opportunity to evolve spiritually will present itself only when I have an earth-life. For it is only then that a person has the opportunity to expend as much of the previous unwholesome *kammic* energy as possible, while at the same time accumulating more and more positive *kammic* energy by way of *dāna-sīla-bhāvanā*: giving-morality-meditation. This is how even the Bodhisattas, [3] over countless rebirths, develop their *pāramitās* (see note 2, chapter 1) and thus spiritually evolve themselves to perfection.

"I could now relate this spiritual evolution to a similar scientific evolution, namely the natural evolution of all animal and plant life. There is sufficient scientific evidence for us to accept the fact that for man to evolve from a single-celled organism to what he is today has taken billions of years. Our spiritual evolution is similar though taking an enormously longer period of time. And, as the Buddha taught, we speak not of years but of *kappas* or eons [4]. Every time we have an earth-life we get the chance to evolve a little spiritually. The extent of this spiritual development depends on the individual person's behaviour in each earth-life. If one commits wrong in this earth life, one will regress. On the other hand, if one does good consistently, then one will evolve progressively a little bit more.

"This is why the Buddhas have repeatedly advised people to, 'refrain from evil, do good deeds and cleanse the mind' (*sabbapāpassa akaraṇaṃ, kusalssa upasampadā, sacittapariyodapanam).* (Dhp. 183)

"I understand that the frequency of an individual's earth-life is based on conditionality and the immanent law of *kamma*. We know from the *Dhamma* that everyone of us will have a manifold number of 'earth-appearances' during our journey in *saṃsāra*. The Buddha has said that even the tears that one has shed on the death of one's parents during one's travels in *saṃsāra* exceed the waters in all the oceans.

"It cannot then be far wrong if the conclusion is reached that all law-abiding, compassionate and kind-hearted individuals have evolved considerably. And that they now have the chance to make a break-through to 'Awakening', should they but apply themselves in accord with the Dhamma. We have developed our individual *pāramitās* to a considerable degree and this is why we have become dedicated *vipassanā* meditators in this life.

"When I picture the end of my previous life in terms of *Paṭiccasamuppāda*, I could see myself in the process of dying. When the final moment of death arrived, there was a microsecond of death-consciousness and the energy of this last consciousness got catalyzed or energized and conditioned the appearance of the first consciousness in the present life—*saṅkhāra-paccayā viññāṇaṃ* (with mental formations as a condition, arises rebirth-consciousness)—thereby ensuring the continuity of the stream of conditioned consciousness in the present life,—*viññāṇa-paccayā nāma-rūpaṃ* (with consciousness as a condition, arises mind-and-body). This conditioned consciousness then became part of the mind-body complex of the current life.

"Prof. Lily de Silva puts it in even simpler terms: 'When ultimately we are on the deathbed face to face with death and our body is no longer strong enough to flee from death, it is highly unlikely that we will mentally accept death with resignation. We will struggle hard, long for and crave for life (*taṇhā*), and reach out and grasp (*upādāna*), a viable base somewhere as the dying body can no longer sustain itself. Once such a viable base in a mother's womb has been grasped, the process of becoming *(bhava)* starts there, which in due course gives rise to birth (*jāti*). This is what is referred to in the twelve-linked *Paṭiccasamuppāda* as "craving conditions grasping, grasping conditions becoming, and becoming conditions birth". Thus a worldling dies and is reborn.' [5]

"On our *saṃsāric* journey, our actions become habitual and these habits become part of our personality and we take these habits with us from life to life in the form of mental formations (*saṅkhāra*) or habit energy. Hence our actions in this life are influenced or conditioned by the habits we had developed over countless previous lives. (Do I see here the embryo of a developing conscience?) I now understood the reason for some of my previous erratic actions that were not consonant with my usual cultivated way of life. Here let me recall similar incidents of errant behaviour by certain monks and laypersons during the time of the Buddha.

"There was once an arahant who instead of gently stepping across tiny water channels in rice-fields when proceeding on alms-rounds with other monks to a nearby village, would simply jump across the obstructions in an undignified manner. This was brought to the notice of the Buddha, who then told the assembly of monks that this arahant had in previous births been born as a monkey and this was the reason for this otherwise unaccountable behaviour.

"In another instance, an arahant frequently addressed other bhikkhus in a disparaging manner using epithets employed at that time by the higher castes in addressing outcasts. Here too, the Buddha attributed it to force of habit from past lives as an affluent Brahmin[6] landowner (Dhp. 408).

"There was an instance where a Brahmin and his wife greeted the Buddha as their son. The Buddha attributed this intimacy to numerous past associations (Dhp. 225).

"In the Upanisā Sutta (Nidāna Saṃy.23) the Buddha explained how once rain starts eroding a mountain, future rains will continue the process till such time when rivulets are formed, and the rivulets gradually create a channel which next forms into streams and next into a river through a process of repeated erosion. All future rains will follow the path of the river, which had been made by repeated erosion. It is in a similar way that our actions become habitual and these habits become part of our personality. We take these habits with us from life to life in the form of mental formations (*saṅkhāra*) or habit energy in our *saṃsāric* journey. Thus, even in this life, an individual is making wholesome and unwholesome *kamma* continuously with every thought, word and deed, thereby adding to or subtracting from the inherited bundle of *kammic* energy, for the Buddha has said:

"Attanā va kataṃ pāpaṃ, attanā saṅkilissati
Attanā akataṃ pāpaṃ attanā va visujjhati
Suddhi asuddhi paccataṃ n' añño aññaṃ visodhaye.

"By committing wrong, one defiles oneself
By not doing wrong, one purifies oneself.
Purity and impurity depends on oneself, no one
purifies another. (Dhp. 165)

"I would then often reflect on the importance of taming the mind. The Buddha has pointed out that 'the mind is very hard to perceive, extremely subtle and goes wherever it wishes' (Dhp. 36), and asks us to guard it. He would often simply refer to the mind as consciousness. Both are often used as synonymous terms. Mind is frequently described as consisting of fleeting mental states which constantly arise and perish with lightning rapidity. 'With birth as its source and death as its mouth, it persistently flows on like a river receiving from its tributaries a stream of constant accretions to its flood.' Each momentary consciousness of this ever-changing life-stream, on passing away, transmits its whole energy to its successor. Each and every consciousness therefore consists of the potentialities of its predecessors and something more, and all its potentialities in the form of conditioned energy are transmitted from life to life.

"I recollect that the Abhidhamma explains the philosophy of the mind by dividing the mental process into two general categories: one as passive consciousness, and the other as active consciousness. Passive consciousness consists of a succession of momentary mental states of a uniform but conditioned nature, called the life-continuum (*bhavaṅga*). This type of consciousness is reported as running through and beneath the whole existence of an individual from birth to death, interrupted only by the occasions of active consciousness. The life-continuum is a result of *kamma* generated in the past existence, which determines the basic disposition of the present individual. This information also helped me to visualize and comprehend with insight for the first time, the *viññāṇa-paccayā nāma-rūpaṃ* (with consciousness as a condition arises mind and body), of *Paṭiccasamuppāda.*

"I can now understand how humankind is beset by greed, hatred and delusion (*loba-dosa-moha*), for we have two sets of factors in our makeup. First, we have the genetic predispositions arising from the genes that we have inherited from our parents. The other is the 'habits' that we have inherited from previous births in the form of *kammic* predispositions, common traits, which we all carry in our evolutionary journey involving the struggle for existence. This is the instinctive desire, just like in other animals, to place oneself above the rest, and to do so one develops a strong sense of individuality, of an 'I', an ego, a need for this 'I' to be selfish and greedy, if one is to survive. Hence the perpetuation of the delusion of 'I' as a separate ego-entity.

"We can then appreciate the fact that people are constantly subject to the negativities or defilements of greed, hatred and delusion. Man, during his evolution from a single-celled organism has, over billions of years struggled to adapt, to compete, to evolve and to survive by whatever possible means, and only the ones who could perpetuate the species best have survived. This has resulted ultimately in the evolving human prototype passing on from generation to generation the inherent tendency towards selfishness and greed. Similarly, over these millions of years, the evolving man has come to think of himself as unique and that each individual was a distinct personality, or 'I', who came first, then the family, next the tribe and so on. These values became part of our genetic make-up, which even today, after a prolonged period of 'civilizing influence', has a tendency to crop up unexpectedly. The only saving grace is our ability to restrain ourselves to keep in line with what society and our very own conscience dictates.

"We could perhaps accept the fact that if our parents were persons who had inherited good spiritual traits from their ancestors, we in turn would have inherited these 'good' genes. If we now live in a social environment that is conducive to good behaviour, we would generally be well-behaved persons. Second, we are also under the influence of our inherited dispositions from our previous travels in *saṃsāra*, and if we had been consistently cruel persons in previous births, this latent tendency ('habit energy') could spring into action and prevent us from behaving better in the present.

"This seems to suggest that we are in effect split personalities because of our inclinations based on our current genes on the one hand and our 'habit-energy' from previous lives, on the other. This is more apparent in some than in others. Remember the fictitious Dr Jekyll and Mr Hyde, and the actual case of

Albert de Salvo, the "Boston Strangler", who turned out to be a mild-mannered family person in normal life? When we understand this and reflect on it during meditation we can come to terms with our latent tendencies (*anusaya*), hidden in the deep unconscious which will unaccountably surface and surprise us in moments when we are not mindful. With this knowledge I learnt to be equanimous (*upekkhā*), and to move onward.

"I continued repeatedly and constantly to meditate on *Paṭiccasamuppāda.* Then I saw with insight that all this time my perceptions of phenomena had been at fault for, instead of perceiving phenomena as coming into being because of 'conditioned arising' and therefore devoid or empty of self, my perception had been that phenomena were existent and real.

"Then it happened one day. I was sitting in mindful meditation with an open yet quiet mind reflecting and contemplating the Buddha's advice to Bāhiya as well as Sāriputta's advice to Anāthapiṇḍika. (ch 4). It then dawned on me that there was possibly yet another and more pertinent and deeper meaning in these instructions. This meaning had perhaps previously eluded me.

"Now by placing myself first in the position of Bāhiya and then Anāthapiṇḍika, I could see clearly with insight that, in the supramundane sense, there is no real person or 'I' involved in the seeing and what are cognized by the senses are only formations subject to causes and conditions. That 'letting go' was for the mind to let go of the very idea that the aggregates (all five of them) are substantial and permanent, and to realize that they are in fact nothing but formations which are subject to the three truths of appearing, momentarily existing and dying (*uppāda, ṭhiti, bhaṅga*).

"It was because my mind was clouded by remnants of greed, hatred and delusion that the true nature of things had been obscured and my perceptions, too, had been incorrect. Although I knew theoretically the truth about our perceptions, and in fact could discuss the subject with my fellow meditators, I had not totally accepted it. The truth was thus revealed through the progressive development of wisdom, which resulted from reading, reflecting and, finally, by insight meditation—*sutamaya,* then *cintāmaya* and finally *bhāvanāmaya paññā.*

"I now became quite excited, for it seemed to me that I had achieved something special. 'Was I now on the Path?' I asked myself. But logical and equanimous thinking intervened. Introspective meditation was what was needed now. Then I forced myself to slow down and look inwards with equanimity and with an open mind. With much reflection I realized that while I had seen phenomena in the proper perspective and come to the proper conclusions, dwelling on them with attachment would simply make them *vipassanā-upakkilesa* or one of the 'imperfections of insight' [7] which I knew about, and which I had often explained to meditators who had been associated with me in group meditation sessions. Here, my own experience was unnecessarily exciting me! The important thing now was to free myself from being deceived and to move forward diligently.

"Now, with further contemplation, I can see that neither one nor all of the five aggregates which make up a person, and any activities (phenomena) resulting therefrom, are anything but mere formations which arise, stay awhile and disintegrate; but under the influence of delusion appear to have an individuality of their own, just as with a mirage where there is an illusion of water, which when approached turns out to be nothing. Neither a self or 'I' was involved in the process— only a continuity of conditioned phenomena occurring in a causal chain. Now I could see that even this present thought is impermanent, for it too will pass away before my very eyes, yielding place to another thought, and yet another, and so on. Hence, accepting every pain, every pleasure, every emotion, every delusion as 'mine', as a permanent 'I' was just a mirage, an illusion,—for they are simply phenomena occurring in a causal chain. The words 'mine' and 'I' therefore are only for use in the conventional sense. Thus, what previously was merely theoretical knowledge now became experiential knowledge. Mundane truths had taken on a new dimension and now become supramundane truths.

"I proceeded to return once again to my reflection and contemplation of the links of the *Paṭiccasampuppāda* both in the forward and the reverse directions with total concentration and immersion. I could see with insight wisdom what was previously mere theoretical knowledge, namely, the truth of both impermanence–*anicca,* and non-self–*anatta*, and that this continued travelling in *saṃsāra* was painful, distressing and unsatisfactory. This elusive breakthrough came in a 'flash' of intuition–of understanding with insight.

" ...Then felt I like some watcher of the skies
When a new planet swims into his ken ..."

John Keats (1795-1821)

"I commenced to experience an indescribable feeling of calm, peace and serenity. When I came out of this state much later, it was with the insight knowledge and acceptance of the reality that 'I' and 'my' are but conventional terms for mere formations. No phenomena, whether mental, or occurring in the external world, are permanent, nor is there a permanent self to be found anywhere. With the dawning of this comprehension, I am now relatively free of the assumption, the sense, and the delusion of a permanent and continuing 'self' travelling in *saṃsāra.*

"I can see that 'habit energy' or the stream of conditioned consciousness *(bhavaṅga)* can be compared to a 'house-guest' occupying this present body. Now, with *paññā* and equanimity I can distance myself from the mundane activities of the present body. It is now possible, with a proper disposition and continuous application supported by equanimity towards all formations, to find a sense of the quietness of the supra-mundane. When some negativity yet surfaces unexpectedly, it is recognized as one which had remained dormant and embedded in the deep unconscious as *anusaya.* I then automatically 'let go' of it with equanimity.

"In time, insight meditation took on a new dimension, for the focus now shifted to Nibbāna and the three characteristics of the human condition, namely impermanence, distress and the absence of a permanent 'I'. One now feels peaceful and relaxed when meditating.

"My understanding of the interconnectedness in the links of *Paṭiccasamuppāda* is now more meaningful because phenomena follow phenomena until the truth is seen. Now, with insight into 'non-self', I find a great reduction in clinging and craving and the mental processes of *viññāṇa-saññā-vedanā-saṅkhāra* now stop before *saṅkhāra* and are replaced by *saṅkhāra-upekkhā.*[8] Then one's mind-processes could now be shown as:

viññāṇa (consciousness)
↓
saññā (perception)
↓
vedanā (sensations)
↓
saṅkhāra-upekkhā (equanimity towards all formations).

"Consequently, one abandons craving and clinging as of no consequence. With this paradigm shift, the inclination, the energy for existence fades away and at this stage all the *kammic* energy begins to diminish automatically.

"This means that from now on, I will be constantly aware that all formations are subject to impermanence, distress and are impersonal. There is only the observation of all phenomena with equanimity. I now have much composure and feel peaceful and comfortable. There is now no occasion to react to incidents in the daily mundane life.

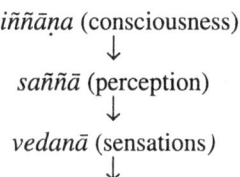

"That I was able to move from *vipassanā upakkilesa* finally to *saṅkhāra-upekkhā-ñāṇa,* marked for me the real breakthrough. But I realize that my task is not yet complete. There is more work to be done. I know that my dedicated goal will eventually be reached as a matter of course. I do not need to yearn for it, for I am confident that this will come to pass when the conditions are ripe.

"When I now focus with insight on the ten fetters (*saṃyojana*) of

1. personality view
2. doubt
3. clinging to rules and rituals as a way to liberation
4. sensual desire
5. illwill or aversion
6. passion for earthly life
7. desire for existence in the Brahma or Formless worlds
8. pride or conceit
9. self-righteousness and finally,
10. ignorance,

that bind a person to *saṃsāra*, I know which of them are not present in me and which of the rest need to be eliminated. I am aware that by continuing the practice of the Noble Eightfold Path, and by way of constant insight meditation on the three characteristics of existence, namely impermanence, distress and non-self, all of these fetters will eventually be eliminated slowly but surely.

"Now let me leave you with a riddle, which you should be able to solve with reflection and contemplation. It may in fact, perhaps, even push you from thinking of liberation to liberation itself!

"Mere suffering exists, no sufferer is found;[9]
The deeds are, but no doer of the deeds is there;
Nirvāṇa is, but not the man who enters it;
The Path is, but no traveller on it is seen."

Vis. XVI*

"Thank you for listening patiently to me."

The above experiences of a Knowledgeable meditator should serve as a source of inspiration to all of us. Readers will observe that he had passed through various stages of insight wisdom leading to what is called "the knowledge of equanimity towards formations"—*sankhara-upekkhā ñāṇa* (see below), and, perhaps, toeven more, which he does not divulge.

According to Srī Ñāṇārāma,[10] "this *saṅkhāra-upekkhā* results from a conviction that all the foundational work for uprooting the defilements has been accomplished and that no further effort is required in this direction. The knowledge of this form of equanimity arises with the understanding of voidness (*suññatā*): that every thing is void of self or what belongs to self. Since the meditator sees that there is neither a self nor anything belonging to a self in relation to himself as well as others, voidness is discerned. There is equanimity at this stage because the meditator understands objects in terms of the four elements."[11]

For further understanding of this critical stage in mental development, we find much information in the *Paṭisambhidāmagga*, which defines the knowledge of equanimity

---

* (Please read note 9 *only* after you have spent a week or two in reflection and contemplation of the above passage.)

about formations in the following manner: "Wisdom consisting of desire for deliverance together with reflection and composure is the 'Knowledge of Equanimity about Formations." According to this definition, *saṅkhāra-uppekkhā* has three stages: (1) desire for deliverance, (2) reflection and (3) composure. Composure is a significant characteristic of equanimity about formations. It implies the continuity of knowledge or the occurrence of a series of knowledges as an unbroken process. For a meditator who has reached this stage, very little remains to be done."

The meditator had been contemplating the three characteristics of all formations as impermanent, suffering and devoid of self—*anicca-dukkha-anatta*. As he continues reflecting on these characteristics with insight, one of the three characteristics stands out more prominently than the others. Which one stands out depends on his dominant spiritual faculty. One is then considered to have reached insight leading to emergence. This applies to those who have a very strong background knowledge of the *Paṭiccasmuppāda* as well. They too will reach a point where, instead of the focus on all three of the characteristics, the focus automatically shifts on to a single characteristic, which stands out above the others.

One in whom faith is predominant will discern impermanence and subsequently apprehend Nibbāna as the signless (*animitta*). One in whom concentration is predominant will discern the mark of suffering and apprehend Nibbāna as the desireless (*appaṇihita*); and one in whom wisdom is predominant will discern the mark of non-self and subsequently apprehend Nibbāna as voidness (*suññatā*). The particular outstanding characteristic comes up distinctly in the most developed phase of *saṅkkhāra-upekkhā ñāṇa*.

In the previous phase the meditator's mind was focused on formations, and he was seeing formations as impermanent, suffering and non-self. His mind had then automatically let go of formations and taken Nibbāna as its object instead. This change signified the meditator's effort to ensure the occurrence of change-of-lineage-knowledge. It heralds the onset of the supramundane path, which abandons defilements permanently by cutting off their roots, and the attainment of the supramundane path is now assured.

The previously discussed knowledge-of-change-of-lineage would have taken but a few mind-moments, and would have been followed immediately thereafter by the supramundane Path-knowledge, which in turn would have been followed directly by its corresponding fruition. Both the Path-knowledge and Fruition-knowledge take Nibbāna as their object. The Path (*magga*) lasts for only a single moment of consciousness, while fruition (*phala*) occurs for two or three mind-moments.

CHAPTER X

Some Questions and Answers

Several readers of *The Road to Liberation* have written me requesting clarification on certain subjects that had surfaced during the reading of Part 1 of that book as well as during their *vipassanā* meditation practice. In this essay an effort is made to address these issues.

Q 1. In your book (Wheel Publication 450-452), you discussed *Satipaṭṭhāna* rather briefly, although the Buddha himself is reported to have stated that Satipaṭṭhāna is the only way to liberation. Could you please elaborate?

A. The practice of the four-fold 'foundations of mindfulness' or establishing of 'awareness of mindfulness' called Satipaṭṭhānawas highly praised by the Buddha. Mentioning its importance in the Maha Satipaṭṭhāna Sutta, he called it *ekāyano maggo*—the way pointing only* to the purification of beings, for overcoming sorrow, for the extinguishing of suffering, for realizing the path of truth and the experiencing of Nibbāna. This is the real meaning of the two Pali words *ekāyano maggo,—that*

---

* Translating these words as "the only way" as traditionalists frequently do is, I think, misleading and not justified.

it points the way (to no other place but) only to Nibbāna. For the Buddha has shown us elsewhere alternate pathways to Nibbāna.

In this sutta the Buddha has presented a practical method for developing experiential knowledge of oneself by means of *kāyānupassanā* (mindful observation of the body), *vedanānupassanā* (mindful observation of sensations), *cittānupassanā* (mindful observation and awareness of the mind) and *dhammānupassanā* (mindful observation and awareness of the contents of the mind). To explore the truth about ourselves, we must examine the reality of what we are—both body and mind. We must learn to observe these within ourselves. Accordingly, we need to keep three points in mind:

1. The reality of the body may be imagined by contemplation, but to experience it directly one must work with body-sensations (*vedanā*) arising within it.
2. Similarly, working with the contents of the mind one attains the actual experience of the mind.
3. Mind and matter are so closely inter-related that the contents of the mind always manifest themselves as sensations in the body.

Therefore, observation of sensations offers a means of examining the totality of our being, physical as well as mental. This strong emphasis on body sensations is because they work as a direct avenue for the attainment of fruition (Nibbāna) by means of 'strong dependence conditions'—*upanissaya-paccayena paccayā.* Thus, when sensations are experienced properly, these become the nearest dependent condition for our liberation.

We can say that there are four dimensions to our nature; the body, sensations, mind, and its contents. These are the avenues for the establishing of awareness in *satipaṭṭhāna*. In order that the observations are complete, it is necessary to experience every facet by means of *vedanā.* This experience of truth will remove the delusions we have about ourselves. In order to come out of the delusion about the world outside, we need to explore how the outside world interacts with our own mind-and-matter phenomenon i.e., our own being, for the outside world comes into contact with us only at the six sense doors: the eye, ear, nose, tongue, body, and mental base. Since all of these sense-doors are contained in the body (*rūpa*), every contact of the outside world is at the body level.

The Buddha, having learned to examine the depths of his own mind, realized that between the external objects and the mental reaction of craving is a missing link, which is feeling or sensations (*vedanā*). Thus, whenever we encounter an object through the five physical senses and the mind, a sensation arises. If the sensation is pleasant we crave to prolong it, if unpleasant, we crave to be rid of it. It is in the chain of Dependent Origination (*Paṭiccasamuppāda*) that the Buddha has expressed this profound discovery:

...Salāyatana-paccayā phasso
Phassapaccayā vedanā
Vedanā-paccayā taṇhā...

"Dependent on the six-sense-spheres, arises contact,
Dependent on contact arises sensation,
Dependent on sensation arises craving..."

Thus the immediate cause for the arising of craving, and consequently of suffering (*dukkha*), is not something outside of us but rather the sensations (*vedanā*) that arise within us.

However, merely awareness of the sensations within us is not enough to remove our delusions. It is essential also to understand the three universal characteristics *(trilakkhaṇa)* of all phenomena in the world, for we must directly experience within ourselves the truth of impermanence, suffering and non-self. This is possible by meditating the *Satipaṭṭhāna* and *Paṭiccasamuppāda* way.

The Mahā Satipaṭṭhāna Sutta (D.22) begins with the observation of the body. Here, under *kāyānupassanā,* several different starting points are explained: observing the in-and-out breath, attention to body movements etc. Thereafter, we progressively develop mindful awareness of sensations, thoughts and mental objects—*vedanānupassanā, cittānupassananā* and *dhammānupassanā.* However, no matter from which point the journey starts, there are 'stations' which everyone must pass through on the way to the final goal. These are described in important sentences repeated at the end of each section. Namely:

Samudaya-dhammānupassī va viharati
Vaya-dhammānupassī va viharati
Samudaya-vaya-dhammānupassī va viharati

"One dwells observing the phenomenon of arising.
One dwells observing the phenomenon of passing away.
One dwells observing the phenomenon of arising and of passing away".

These sentences reveal the essence of the practice of *sati-paṭṭhāna* meditation, for when these three levels of *anicca* are directly experienced, we will develop the requisite wisdom, which leads to detachment and liberation.

Q 2. In *vipassanā* meditation under *kāyānupassanā*, one of the subjects we are asked to reflect on is the repulsive nature of the body. Could you please elaborate?

A. In answering the previous question, I mentioned that there are four main topics for exploration and development of self-knowledge by development of insight. The first of these was *kāyānupassanā* or observation of the body, and within this body contemplation, the Buddha had recommended insight meditation on the following:

Awareness of respiration,
Awareness of postures of the body,
Constant and thorough understanding of impermanence, and
Reflection on the repulsiveness of the body.

In regard to the last of the above four subjects, the translation of the text reads as follows:

> "Again, O monks, a monk reflects on this very body, that it is covered with skin and full of impurities of all kinds from the soles of the feet upwards and from the hair of the head downwards, considering thus: 'In this body there are hairs of the head, body hairs, nails, teeth, skin, flesh, sinews, bones, bone-marrow, kidney, heart, liver, diaphragm, spleen, lungs, intestines, mesentery, stomach with its contents, faeces, bile, phlegm, pus, blood, sweat, fat, tears, lubricants, saliva, nasal mucous, synovial fluid, urine and the brain.'

> "Just as if there were a double-mouthed provision bag, full of various kinds of grains and seeds, such as hill-paddy rice, paddy-rice, mung-beans, cow-peas, sesame seeds and husked rice and as if there were a man with good eyesight, who, after having opened that bag would examine the contents saying: 'This is hill paddy-rice, this is paddy-rice, these are mung-beans, these are cow-peas, these are sesame seeds and this is husked rice.'
>
> "In the same way, O monks, a monk reflects on this very body, that is covered with skin and ... urine and brain.'
>
> "He thus abides observing body within body internally, or he abides observing body within body both internally and externally. Thus he abides observing the phenomenon of arising in the body, thus he observes the phenomenon of passing away in the body, and thus he abides observing the phenomenon of simultaneous arising-and-passing-away in the body. Awareness that, 'This is body' remains present in him. Thus he develops the awareness to such an extent that there is mere understanding along with mere awareness. In this way he abides detached, without clinging, or craving towards anything in this world of mind and matter. This is how, monks, a monk abides observing body within body".

The Buddha has also described these thirty-two parts of the body and the related simile in the Kāyagatānussati Sutta (M.119) as well as in various other suttas.

The perception of bodily attractiveness lasts only as long as the body is looked at superficially and grasped in terms of selected impressions. To counter this perception, it is necessary to constantly meditate on the body by visualizing the distasteful aspects of the components of the body with comprehension and full awareness of their distastefulness. The desire, the lust, and the passion will then disappear. The meditator takes one's own body as an object and using visualization as an aid, one mentally dissects the body into its component parts and looks at them one by one, focusing on their repulsive nature. The text mentions thirty two parts: head-hairs, body-hairs, finger and toe-nails, teeth, skin, flesh, sinews, bones, bone-marrow, kidneys, heart, liver, diaphragm, spleen, lungs, large intestines, mesentery, stomach contents, excrement, bile, phlegm, pus, blood, sweat, fat, tears, lubricants, snot, phlegm, sinovial fluid, urine and the brain. The aim of this meditation must not be misunderstood. *The aim is not to produce aversion and disgust, but only detachment so as to be able to extinguish the fire of lust.*

This meditation is popular in South-East Asia, and is commonly referred to as *asubha bhāvanā* — "distasteful meditation subject". Alternatively, it is often referred to in the West as the meditation on a "woman or man, as a bag of bones".

A meditation teacher will often give this *asubha bhāvanā* as the subject for meditation at an early stage of a *vipassanā* meditation course to those students whom he reckons are sensually inclined.

In this context, I cannot help but relate an incident that was reported to have happened in the past. A certain conscientious meditating monk was walking one night along the road to his temple when a woman fully adorned with jewelry, earrings and anklets passed by grinning and laughing. A short while later her husband came rushing along the road and seeing the monk asked him whether he had seen a well-dressed young woman, and he then described the woman, her dress and ornaments. The monk replied that he saw no such woman, but that a skeleton with bright teeth had passed by sometime previously! The fact was that the monk had been totally immersed in the meditation on the *asubha bhāvanā* and he saw only the gleaming white teeth (the fourth of the thirty-two body parts) listed in that meditation subject!

Q 3. Can you briefly summarize contemplative meditation on *Paṭiccasamuppāda*?

A. This could be considered critically the most important part of our study, cessation or deliverance from the round of birth and rebirth. To begin our quest to understand cessation, we can practise with insight, the two-fold forward and reverse contemplation of the twelve links of dependent origination, which are: ignorance, mental formations, consciousness, mind and body, the six sense faculties, contact, feeling, craving, grasping, existence, birth, and death and decay.

Forward contemplation throws light on the existence of suffering, leading to the question, "What is the origin of suffering?". Following the causal chain of existence, we first contemplate how fundamentally does ignorance set in motion the life cycle. Ignorance then conditions action, and actions condition consciousness. From consciousness we contemplate name-and-form, and then on to the six sense-faculties and so forth until we finally see that our desire leads to grasping. Because there is grasping, there is becoming which leads to birth. Finally, we become subject to sickness, mental and physical pain, ageing and ultimately to death.

The realization of birth, existence, decay and death (*uppāda, ṭhiti, bhaṅga*) of every activity, leads to a profound understanding of the unenviable state in which we find ourselves. This is the forward contemplation of the twelve links of *Paṭiccasamuppāda*, and its purpose, as was stated previously, is to help us realize cessation.

When we practise reverse contemplation (i.e., on the absense of *dukkha*) , we can realize emptiness. Here too we begin with initial ignorance *(avijjā),* and contemplate by asking ourselves the question as to what occurs when there is no ignorance? And we see the answer, namely, that there will not be any deluded actions. Once there are no deluded actions, there is then no defilement of consciousness. We proceed in this fashion onto the six sense faculties which give rise naturally to contact, desire, grasping, existence, birth, death and so on. This is the reverse contemplation on the cessation of the twelve-linked chain of dependent origination.

However, what is most important is to understand fully the reality of the fundamental ignorance with which we enter the world. In Buddhism *avijjā* means a misconception, a misjudgement of the nature of the world. Specifically, it means not understanding the three facts of existence which are: imper-manence (*anicca*), suffering *(dukkha)* and non-self (*anatta*).

We thus have forward contemplation on the cause of *dukkha*, and the reverse contemplation on the non-existence of *dukkha*. In the forward contemplation we realize how we come into being and in the reverse we realize that we have no independent self. It must be remembered that both modes of contemplation are related and it is necessary to complement one with the other. It is with this dual approach that we can truly comprehend cessation with insight, and so terminate our wandering in *saṃsāra*.

When we awaken to the true nature of things, our mind will be free of *avijjā*. It will be illuminated with wisdom, and by transcending ignorance we will no longer be conditioned by it. This non-conditioning will then become true for the remaining links of the chain one after another, thereby terminating birth-and-death.

Our ignorant belief that things are real is extremely powerful. But we should remember that this is nothing but an error in judgement. It is merely a delusion that we cling to, but which in fact has no foundation whatsoever. On the other hand, its opposite, the understanding that phenomena have no reality, is based on a consistent truth that stands up to investigation. If one familiarizes oneself with this understanding, it can be developed indefinitely, since it is both a true and a natural quality of the mind. It is through insight meditation that we can establish firmly the view of emptiness, and with it completely destroy the veils that obscure true knowledge.

Let us recollect that the Buddha presented the teaching on emptiness to his original band of five monks, by way of the Anattalakkhaṇa Sutta (Khanda Samy. 59) in which he pointed out to them that every phenomenon was devoid a "self" (Ch. 4 in in Part 1, *The Road to Liberation*).

The emptiness of substantial reality is called "non-self". Those who realize the nature of emptiness also realize that their own nature is that of flux, change and impermanence. They directly experience that mind, body and environment are pervaded with a dynamic quality of emptiness. A first inkling of this emptiness comes to one who is on the threshold of awakening and is fully realized only when one "enters the stream" as an *Ariya*.

Q 4. What is the position of *Satipaṭṭhāna* vis-a-vis *Paṭiccasamuppāda* and the Four Noble Truths in our insight meditation towards Nibbāna?

A. This is a fundamental question which is quite excellent.

All our efforts in meditation are for the purpose of a gradual evolution of *paññā* or insight wisdom,— *bhāvanāmaya paññā*. Fundamentally, it is to develop experiential knowledge of *anicca, dukkha* and *anatta*—impermanence, distress and non-self. What makes this so difficult is that the human condition is beset by the three negative characteristics of greed, hatred and delusion—*lobha, dosa* and *moha.*

To understand the three factors of impermanence, distress and non-self, requires deep contemplation the *vipassanā* way. It is by focusing on the twelve links of *Paṭiccasamuppāda* that one can come to an experiential understanding of how the human condition comes to be, which with all its weaknesses, contributes to the delusion that there is a permanent entity called a "self." Once we accept this position then we see that greed and hatred become concomitant factors towards its preservation. The Noble Eightfold Path, which is the fourth Noble Truth, teaches us how to develop insight, and it is by meditating according to the directions in the Satipaṭṭhāna Sutta (M.16), that we can experientially observe impermanence and the phenomena of arising, passing away and both arising and passing away. By experiencing *anicca* at these levels, we develop *paññā*—the gateway to equanimity—based on the experience of impermanence. This in turn leads to detachment followed by liberation.

In the case of *Paṭiccasamuppāda*, our repeated contemplation of its twelve factors in both the forward and the reverse directions with *sati-sampajañña* (mindfulness with full awareness) results in detachment and the experience of all the three characteristics of existence, namely *anicca, dukkha* and *anatta*. It is here that a word of caution is merited, for it is only with a paradigm shift indicating that we are living the twelve links of dependent origination that we can come to this true understanding.

Insight meditation on the Four Noble Truths is explained as the fourth part of the Satipaṭṭhāna Sutta (M.16) under *Dhammānupassanā*, commencing with the words; *Puna ca paraṃ bhikkhave, bhikkhu dhammesu dhammānupassī viharati catusu ariyasaccesu…*—meaning: "Again, O monks, a monk abides observing mental contents within mental contents, concerning the Four Noble Truths…"

The interconnectedness of the twelve links of the *Paṭiccasamuppāda,* the Four Noble Truths and the Four Foundations of Mindfulness (*Satipaṭṭhāna*) should thus be self-evident. They all lead to just one goal, namely, liberation – Nibbāna.

Q 5. Could you please explain the step-wise method of *mettā* meditation?

A. Let me explain how to practise this with meditation groups.

If the meditators are Buddhists, we start by first repeating in unison the three refuges, the five precepts and the verses in praise of the Triple Gem as follows:

Namo tassa Bhagavato Arahato Sammā Sambuddhassa (three times)

"Homage to the Blessed One, The Perfect One,
the Fully Awakened One."

The Refuges

Buddhaṃ saraṇaṃ gacchāmi,
Dhammaṃ saraṇaṃ gacchāmi,
Saṅghaṃ saraṇaṃ gacchāmi.
Dutiyampi … gacchāmi,
Tatiyampi … gacchāmi.

"I go to the Buddha for refuge, I go to the Dhamma for refuge and I go to the Sangha for refuge." I go a second and a third time for refuge to the Buddha, the Dhamma and the Sangha."

The Precepts

Pāṇātipātā veramaṇī sikkhāpadaṃ samādiyāmi
Adinnādānā veramaṇī sikkhāpadaṃ samādiyāmi
Kāmesu michācārā veramaṇī sikkhāpadaṃ samādiyāmi
Musāvādā veramaṇī sikkhāpadaṃ samādiyāmi
Surāmerayamajjapamādaṭṭhānā veramaṇī sikkāpadaṃ samādiyāmi.

"I volunteer to abstain from killing and hurting sentient beings;
I volunteer to abstain from stealing;
I volunteer to abstain from sexual misconduct;
I volunteer to abstain from telling lies;
I volunteer to abstain from taking drugs and intoxicants that cause intoxication and heedlessness.

Praise of the Buddha

Iti'pi so Bhagavā arahaṃ, sammā-sambuddho, vijjā-caraṇa-sampanno, sugato, lokavidū, anuttaro purisadammasārathī, satthā devamanussānaṃ, buddho bhagavā'ti.

"Such indeed is the Blessed One: perfected, fully awakened, endowed with knowledge and discipline, having walked the right path, the knower of the worlds, incomparable guide of amenable men and women, teacher of gods and humans, awakened and blessed."

Praise of the Dhamma

Svākkhāto bhagavatā dhammo, sandiṭṭhiko, akāliko, ehipassiko, opanayiko paccattaṃ veditabbo viññūhi'ti.

"Well taught is the doctrine of the Blessed One, of immediate benefit, timeless, inviting us to experience it, leading us onwards, to be comprehended individually by the wise."

Praise of the Saṅgha

Supaṭipanno bhagvato sāvakasaṅgho, ujupaṭipanno bhagavato sāvakasaṅgho, ñāyapaṭipanno bhagavato sāvakasaṅgho, sāmīcipaṭipanno bhagavato sāvakasaṅgho: yadidaṃ cattāri purisayugāni aṭṭhapurisapuggalā, esa bhgavato sāvakasaṅgho, āhuneyyo, pāhuneyyo, dakkhiṇeyyo, añjalikara-ṇīyo anuttaraṃ puññakkhettaṃ lokassā'ti

"Wholesome in conduct is the community of disciples of the Blessed One, honest in conduct is the community of disciples of the Blessed One, wise in conduct is the community of disciples of the Blessed One, proper in conduct is the community of disciples of the Blessed One. These four pairs of persons, eight individuals, this is the community of disciples of the Blessed One:[1] Worthy of offerings and hospitality, gifts and homage, it is an incomparable field of merit for the world."

Reciting these verses while focusing on the meaning of the words helps one to calm the mind and make it pliable for meditation.

On the other hand, if I were meditating with a group of non-Buddhists, I would request all the participants to first gently close their eyes and then to start relaxing all the muscles in the body consciously: begin with the head, then the facial muscles, next those in the neck, and so on until one comes to the toes, until they are fully relaxed and devoid of tensions in body and mind. They are then asked to take one or two breaths consciously and while exhaling say to themselves that all negativities are being expelled with each exhalation.

Mettā Meditation

After a moment of silence, now that they are fully relaxed, I ask them to imagine that there is a rosebud about to bloom where our hearts are. (For Sri Lankans and South-East Asian groups it would be a lotus.) Participants are then asked to imagine that this flower bud is now slowly opening in the morning sun, and that as its petals unfold, the sweet scent of the flower spreads first to its immediate surroundings and then a gentle wind wafts its fragrance farther and farther. I then ask them to fill their hearts with universal kindness or *mettā*, and then release the scent of this goodness slowly so as to fill the entire meditation room, then to spread out to the garden outside, next to cover the entire city, then the State, then the whole country, the whole world, and finally to embrace the entire universe with all its living beings.

We then request one of the participants to lead the rest in repeating a 'wish for happiness'. This could be similar to the one in Wheel, 450-452, or it could be one which the participant had himself formulated. As an alternative I give below an invocation offered by Sondra Jewell, a friend of mine (after attending a *vipassanā* retreat with Ven. Gunaratana Mahā Thera in Canada), which we find quite soothing and appropriate during group meditation sessions.

Loving-Friendliness Meditation

"***May I be healthy.*** May I be happy. May my heart be filled with love. May I be peaceful. May I have ease of well-being. May I live in safety. May no problems come to me. May no difficulties come to me. May no harm come to me. May I always meet with success.

May I have patience, strength, courage, inner clarity and wisdom to meet and overcome inevitable difficulties, problems and failures in life.

May my whole heart be filled with loving-friendliness. May every cell of my body be filled with loving-friendliness. May every level of my consciousness be purified with loving-friendliness. May I build a healthy, happy aura of loving-friendliness all around myself, and may I be protected.

May my parents be healthy. May they be happy. May their hearts be filled with love. May they be peaceful. May they have ease of well-being. May they live in safety. May no problems come to them. May no difficulties come to them. May no harm come to them. May they always meet with success.

May they have patience, strength, courage, inner clarity and wisdom to meet and overcome inevitable difficulties, problems and failures in life.

May their whole hearts be filled with loving-friendliness. May every cell of their body be filled with loving-friendliness. May every level of their consciousness be purified with loving-friendliness. May they build a healthy, happy aura of loving-friendliness all around themselves and may they be protected.

May my teachers be healthy. May… and may they be protected.

May my loved ones be healthy. May… and may they be protected.

May my friends, co-workers and neighbours be healthy. May… and may they be protected.

May those I have harmed, or who have harmed me, be healthy. May … and may they be protected.

May all living beings be healthy. May … and may they be protected." – S.J.

We follow this with five to ten minutes of silent meditation on *mettā* (loving-kindness), as well as *karuṇā* (compassion), for we know that the practical application or consummation of *mettā bhāvanā* (meditation) is by acts of compassion directed towards the deserving.

At the conclusion of the *mettā bhāvanā* session, I would briefly describe the method suggested by the Buddha for developing these sublime states. (See Wheel Publication 450-452, page 100).

Q. 6. Over the last decade, a number of friends of mine and I have attended several ten-day and even monthly retreats at various *vipassanā* training centers. We now do individual meditation as well as regular group meditations. But, while we can reach a satisfactory level of serenity during and after these meditation sessions, a "break-through" to the *Ariya* life eludes us. Why is this?

A. It is not possible to generalize about this kind of situation. I appreciate your question, but there are so many possible problems, permutations and combinations of such problems that a completely satisfactory answer is impossible. It would perhaps have been easier if each of you had discussed your individual problems with your respective meditation masters.

However, I can suggest some questions, which you can ask yourself first. You can use them as a checklist and proceed onwards with confidence, correcting the deficiencies and the day will surely come when, like the "experinced meditator" whose experiences are described in chapter 3 of this book, you will be able to make a break-through from the mundane to the supramundane. Please always remember that everything must be observed, discovered and experienced only in one's body, and nowhere else.

1. Do you spend a sufficient number of hours regularly each day for meditation?

2. Do you practise the five or eight precepts in thought, word and deed at all times?

3. Have you read and understood the Dhamma in such aitushion that you can unhesitatingly understand references to *kamma, kamma-vipāka, anicca-dukkha-anatta, loba-dosa-moha, vipassanā* and so on as explained in Dhamma talks and in this book?

4. Do you understand the twelve links of the *Paṭiccasamuppāda* and their interdependence and conditionality (*paccaya*)?

5. Are you earnestly following the Noble Eightfold Path?

6. Do you see the interconnectedness of *Paṭiccasamuppāda*, the Noble Eightfold Path and the four *Satipaṭṭhānas*?

7. Can you understand fully what is meant by formations, phenomena and conditionality when your meditation master mentions them during lectures?

8. Has your meditation teacher walked you through the twelve links of *Paṭiccasamuppāda* as an intensive meditation subject?
9. Do you spend some time each day meditating on the *brahma-vihāras*? Do you develop and practise them in your daily life?
10. Do you discuss your doubts, and does your meditation teacher clarify them?
11. Do you practise walking meditation in addition to seated meditation daily?
12. Are you equanimous and mindful at all times?

Q. 7. We often hear of "Three Turnings of the Wheel". What does it mean?

A. We come across this in the Mahāyāna tradition and it essentially is not contradicted in the Theravāda suttas. When the Buddha originally proclaimed the Four Noble Truths, which includes the Eightfold Path, to the *Pancavaggiyas* (group of five ascetics), He is supposed to have repeated the exposition of the Dhammacakkappavattana Sutta (Sacca Saṃy. 11) three times. On his first preaching, Kondañña is believed to have become an *Ariya*; with the second; Vappa and Bhaddiya; and with the third turning Assaji and Mahānāma.

According to the Theravada tradition, after his first sermon the Buddha is said to have taught the Dhamma to these five disciples for a period of time. It is said that while three of the disciples went for alms, the Buddha would teach the other two, and when these two went for alms he would teach the other three. It was only when he was fully satisfied that all five could understand and comprehend his Dhamma, that he preached his next sermon, which was the Anattalakkhaṇa Sutta, hearing which all five of them attained *arahanthship*.

Q. 8. I was fascinated after listening to your description of the experiences of an experinced meditator. Do you have other examples of persons who have recently achieved transcendence?

A. Upāsikā Kee Nanayon (1901-1978) was one of the foremost Dhamma teachers of modern Thailand. Her talks, concise and to the point, have provided an enormous number of people with incisive insight into meditative techniques leading to liberation.

The following is what she had to say about herself, without claiming in words that she was an *Ariya*.

> "...One night, I was sitting in meditation outside in the open air—my back straight as an arrow—firmly determined to make the mind quiet, but even after a long time it wouldn't settle down. So I thought, I've been working at this for many days now, and yet my mind won't settle down at all. It's time to stop being so determined and to simply be aware of the mind. I started to take my hands and feet out of the meditation posture, but at the moment I had unfolded one leg but had yet to unfold the other, I could see that my mind was like a pendulum swinging more and more slowly, more and more slowly—until it stopped.
>
> "Then there arose an awareness, which sustained itself. Slowly I put my legs and hands back into position. At the same time, the mind was in a state of awareness absolutely and solidly still, seeing clearly

the elementary phenomena of existence as they arose and disbanded, changing in line with their nature—and also seeing, a separate condition inside, with no arising, disbanding or changing, a condition beyond birth and death: something very difficult to put clearly into words, because it was a realization of the elementary phenomena of nature, completely internal and individual.

"After a while I slowly got up and lay down to rest. This state of mind remained as a stillness, which sustained itself deep down inside. Eventually the mind came out of this state and gradually returned to normal…"

In the above anecdote this meditation teacher shows us how she achieved transcendence when focusing on *Anatta*. (From B.P.S.Wheel No. 373/374)

Q. 9. Could you please summarize for us the Buddha's thinking on conditionality, which in turn leads to his doctrine of Dependent Origination or *Paṭiccasamuppāda*?

A. During the time of the Buddha, there were numerous speculative theories on 'Causation' such as self or internal causation, external causation, a combination of the two, and finally, that things originate due neither to internal or external causes but due to mere chance or accident.

The Buddha carefully examined these theories and found no substance in them. To the contrary, he saw some uniform causal patterns in the world, which could be summarized into four groups, namely:

1. That causation actually takes place in the world. It is an actual happening, but not the work of any person.

2. That as long as certain conditions exist, certain effects are bound to come into being, or even more simply, take place.
3. That under a certain set of conditions (and as long as they remain unchanged), they give rise to certain predictable effects.
4. That for things to come into being, there should be certain conditions (conditionality), thus emphasizing the fact that causation is neither a chance happening nor a pre-determined happening.

The Buddha used the above observations when formulating the theory of origination, cessation and causation, which he summarized as follows:

This general theory of causality explains the origin and cessation of everything in the world. The whole universe (including everything in it) comes within the operation of this principle.

The Buddha's main concern, however, was with regard to man and his experiencing of unsatisfactoriness or distress *(dukkha)*, and his mission was to find an answer leading to the cessation or escape from *dukkha.* It was by applying this general theory of causality that he was able to evolve a specific formula to explain how man continues to travel in *saṃsāra* undergoing distress, and how this journey could be terminated. This formula is what we know as the Dependent Origination or *Paṭiccasamuppāda*. It is as follows:

> 'When this is present that comes to be. On the arising of this that arises. When this is absent, that does not come to be. On the cessa-

> tion of this, that ceases. That is to say: On ignorance depends dispositions or mental formations; on dispositions or mental formations depends consciousness; on consciousness depends name and form or the psycho-physical personality; on name and form depend the six 'gateways' of sense perception; on the six 'gateways' depends contact; on contact depends feeling; on feelings depends desire (craving); on desire depends grasping; on grasping depends becoming; on becoming depends birth; and on birth depends ageing, sorrow, lamentation, suffering, dejection and vexation. In this manner arises a mass of suffering'.

Paṭiccasamuppāda clearly shows that things come into existence through cause and conditions and cease when these causes and conditions are absent. It should, however, be kept in mind that although ignorance is at the head of the list of the twelve factors, it does not mean that it is a *first cause*, for the twelve factors can be considered in the form of a circle or an ever-continuing repetitive chain in which *any of the twelve factors can be used as a starting point.* We also need to remember that in addition to the absence of a first cause, there is also no single cause but only causes and conditions that invariably bring related effects. In fact, *all twelve factors are inter-related, inter-connected.* They are merely causes and conditions that produce effects.

The Buddha used many simple examples to illustrate the nature of dependent origination. He said that the flame in an oil lamp burns "dependent on the oil and the wick". When both of these are present, we see a flame, but if either is absent, the flame will cease to exist. He also used the example of the sprout, which he pointed out, arises dependent on the seed, earth, water, air and light.

Our interest in the principles underlying *Paṭiccasamuppāda* lies in its relationship to the problem of impermanence, distress or unsatisfactoriness (*dukkha*), and rebirth. We are in fact interested in how dependent origination explains the situation in which we find ourselves here and now, and how to free ourselves from this suffering.

Q. 10. Could you tell us briefly the manner in which the Buddha made the greatest of his discoveries?

A. It was on the night of his enlightenment that the Buddha discovered the cause of suffering which he attributed to craving (desire), ill will and delusion (ignorance of *anatta*).

Thus in the Mūlapariyāya Sutta (M.1) he says:

> "Therefore, bhikkhus, through the complete destruction, fading away, cessation, abandoning and relinquishing of cravings, the Thathāgata has awakened to the supreme perfect enlightenment. —What is the reason? Because he has understood that delight is the root cause of suffering, and that with existence (as condition) there is birth, and that for what has come to be there is ageing and death. Therefore, bhikkhus, through the complete destruction, fading away, cessation, abandoning, and relinquishing of all cravings, the Thathāgata has awakened to the supreme perfect enlightenment, I declare".

Elsewhere too the Buddha has said the same thing, that the door to his enlightenment was opened when he saw the cause of suffering as desire, ill will and ignorance. And if we want to be rational in our examination, *we must focus upon ignorance,* because it is due to ignorance that desire and ill will arise.

Essentially, ignorance is the idea of a permanent, independent self. It is this conception of an 'I', opposed to and separate from the people and things around us, that is the root cause of suffering. Once we have the notion of 'I', we have an inclination to favour those things that sustain this 'I' and to be averse to those things that we think threaten this 'I'. It is this conception of the self that is the fundamental cause of suffering, and the root of the various negative emotions such as anger, envy, desire, ill-will, jealousy and greed. To add to the confusion is our ignorance of the fact that in reality there is no such permanent thing as 'I' and that what we label as 'I' is merely a convenient name given to a collection of ever-changing, dependently originating factors or aggregates. The 'self' then is just a convenient name for a collcction of processes.

In this context the self is compared to a rope, which in the dark may be mistaken for a snake, thus causing fear. Similarly, in the darkness of ignorance, we take the impersonal processes of feelings (*vedanā*), perception (*saññā*) and so forth to be a self. As a result we desire certain things and we are averse to others. So ignorance in this sense is the mistaken notion of a permanent ego (*atta*) as a real self.

It is only when this egotism is removed or dispelled by right understanding (which in turn is possible only with insight meditation) that greed, anger and delusion become things of the past and the end of suffering is gained.

Q. 11. We now hear a lot about emptiness and voidness. Could you please explain?

A. True cessation is the full realization of the nature of emptiness (egolessness) and the liberation of oneself from the cycle of birth-and-death. How does one fully realize the nature of emptiness (*suññatā*)? To understand emptiness we need to first understand the working of causes and conditions as was explained previously. Phenomena come into being through "conditioned arising", the coming together of causes and conditions mutually influencing one another. Everything is in a state of constant flux. Nothing remains the same one instant to the next. Through this constant transformation all phenomena arise, change and eventually cease. Since everything is in flux without a permanent nature or identity, there can be no separately identifiable "self". This condition is known as the phenomenon of "emptiness".

The Dalai Lama[2] has explained emptiness as follows: "All phenomena are by nature empty, devoid of true existence. But what is our perception of phenomena at the moment? What we experience is just the opposite. Rather than perceiving phenomena as empty, we see everything as existent and real. It is only through study and practice that we gain some understanding and confidence that the nature of things is emptiness. Then we realize that our perceptions hitherto have not corresponded at all to the way things really are and that we ignorantly cling to our mistaken way of seeing things."

It is this ignorance, which is at the root of desire and hatred. In other words, it is the very root cause of our travels in *saṃsāra*.

There is a saying which is quite apt here:

Thirty spokes converge upon a single hub,
It is on the hole in the centre
that the use of the cart hinges:
We make a vessel from a lump of clay,
It is the empty space within the vessel
that makes it useful.
We make doors and windows for a room,
But it is these empty spaces that make the room liveable.
Thus, while the tangibles have advantages,
It is the intangible that makes it useful.

Q. 12. Why do we need to realize emptiness? And how?

A. We need to realize emptiness because we do not wish to suffer and we know that the root cause of suffering is the untamed mind. Because the mind perceives and understands things mistakenly, negative emotions arise and the mind is never at peace. To avoid this, we must develop the mind so that it perceives the true nature of phenomena. It is because of our mistaken perception that we fail to see things as they really are.

Much of what we perceive is perceived in a mistaken way, seeing things not as they truly are. This is how we become deluded. To avoid this, we should not accept our perceptions in the way we experience them. We should rather analyze and investigate whether we are seeing things as they truly are or not.

The mind's ignorant clinging to things and its subsequent way of functioning obscure our vision regarding the true nature of things. Thus, relative truth is based on the findings of the mind that examines things in a conventional way. If we analyze further and try to see the true nature of phenomena, we can find the ultimate nature of reality. Here we distinguish between the way things appear (relative truth) and the way they really are (absolute truth), which is what is perceived by the non-deluded mind. The absolute truth is revealed through the development of wisdom, which in turn is evelopedthrough skillful listening, reflecting and insight meditation. When one investigates the nature of the individual and of all phenomena, one finds that their nature is emptiness. This emptiness is an absolute truth that is apparent to the mind. One can see it with one's awareness—*sati-sampajañña*. Once it has been experienced, it is not necessary to demonstrate it again. By referring to one's experience of this nature, one can recall it. Its existence is true, and one does not have to rely on argument to prove that it exists. This absolute nature is established through the three stages of evolutionary development of wisdom—*sutamaya paññā, cintāmaya paññā*—and *bhāvanā-maya paññā* by listening, reflecting and meditation. It is something that we can experience.

The Dalai Lama explains further: "However, when one looks for this emptiness, and tries to find where it is, one cannot find it. Its nature is nonexistence, for it is not something that can be analyzed and discovered. To take an example, we can say that a vase has the nature of emptiness, but when we look for the emptiness, it is nonexistent. All we can find is the emptiness of emptiness, but we cannot find emptiness. What has been found by experiencing it through listening, reflecting and meditating cannot be found other than experientially".

This is the important point. For, the understanding and experiencing of this truth comes only by progression or development of wisdom along the path of listening (or reading), reflecting and meditating.

Q. 13. Some speak of time and space in relation to the Dhamma. What does it mean?

A. The Four Noble Truths show us two kinds of cause-and-effect principles at work. One can be called "worldly-cause-and effect", which leads to suffering, and the other "transcendent cause-and-effect", which leads to liberation.

Worldly cause-and-effect takes place in space and time and whatever exists in space and time is characterized by impermanence. Yesterday you were not listening to me; today you are doing so; and after listening you will probably not reflect on it for some time. What we experience here is impermanence. This sense of change also gives us a sense of continuity in our lives. But let us not forget that as the days go by, our lives are also coming to a close, day by day. So impermanence is essentially this progression from birth to death, from existence to non-existence.

To experience impermanence we must exist in the space-time continuum. Our sense of space can be great or small. What is different is the key to how we experience the workings of causes and conditions. The different factors coming together and dispersing give us a sense of time. The very fact that the different aspects of our lives shift, alter and transform, results from these causal relationships. The workings of cause and conditions, which take place in space, are inseparable and imbedded in time, so we experience time and space together. And this experience of constant change is impermanence.

Simply put, world transcendence is freedom from worldly cause-and-effect, freedom from suffering in time and space. The awakened or liberated ones—the arahats, are no longer fettered by time-and-space, and therefore no longer influenced by the suffering which impermanence brings. The state of world-transcendence is a state of liberation.

Q. 14. How do the worldly and world-transcending realities relate to the Four Noble Truths?

A. Worldly cause-and-effect encompasses the first two Noble Truths of suffering and the origination of suffering. Suffering is actually an effect of living in time and space, and its origin is our ignorance (first factor in *Paṭiccasamuppāda*).

World-transcending cause-and-effect relates to the third and fourth of the Four Noble Truths of the cessation of suffering and the path that leads out of suffering. Cessation is the state in which worldly cause-and-effect is abandoned, there is no more accumulation of *kamma*, and liberation is realized. Thus, when the Buddha taught the doctrines of *Paṭiccasamuppāda* and of the Four Noble Truths, he also taught that the path of liberation is the path of moving from the worldly to the world-transcending modes of acting, thinking and speaking.

CHAPTER XI

The Suttas and Transcendence

When we survey the Sutta Piṭaka, we find a number of suttas which, when comprehended with insight, have inspired many a meditator to directly achieve liberation. We are no doubt familiar with the fact that at the very first preaching of the Dhammacakkappavattana Sutta (Sacca Saṃy. 11), Koṇḍañña "saw the eye of the *dhamma*" and became a *sotāpanna*. According to legend, two more of the original five bhikkhus (*pañcavaggiya*) became *sotāpannas* when he repeated to them this sutta, and the last two similarly became stream-winners when he repeated this sutta to them for the third time. In Mahāyāna literature these are called the 'three turnings of the Wheel" of the Dhamma. As stated elsewhere in this current presentation, it is said that when the Buddha preached his second sermon, the Anattalakkhaṇa Sutta, all five of them reached liberation and became arahants. The Salāyatana Saṃyutta too is replete with examples of individual monks achieving liberation at the end of one-on-one discussions with the Buddha.

Serious advanced meditators would also be aware of the fact that comprehension of *Paṭiccasamuppāda* with insight wisdom through *vipassanā* meditation can be a direct route to transcendence, for the Buddha has said in the Satipaṭṭhāna Sutta (M.16):

"He who sees dependent origination sees the dhamma, he who sees the dhamma sees dependent origination".

And at the end of the Mahā Satipaṭṭhāna Sutta (D.22), the Buddha says: "Indeed, O monks, whoever practises this fourfold establishing of awareness in exactly this manner for seven years ... let alone seven months ... let alone half a month, O monks ... for seven days, one of two results can be expected in him: highest wisdom or, aware of a substratum of aggregates remaining, the stage of non-returner."

For the convenience of advanced *vipassanā* meditators, I wish to discuss below a few of the popular suttas, an intensive study of which can provide the background material for the development of insight wisdom that will lead them, when conditions are ripe, to transcendence. In each case, I propose to briefly point out the most significant aspects from my limited comprehension. It is left to the meditator to apply himself thereafter in the appropriate fashion of contemplation and reflection to achieve his goal.

The Anattalakkhaṇa Sutta (Khanda Samy. 59)

On one occasion the Exalted One was dwelling at the Deer park in Isipathana, near Benares. Then the Exalted One addressed the band of five bhikkhus, saying, "O bhikkhus!" "Ven. sir," they replied. Thereupon the Exalted One spoke as follows:

"The body (*rūpa*), O bhikkhus, is soulless (*anatta*). If, O bhikkhus, there were in this a soul, then this body would not be subject to suffering. 'Let this body be thus, let this body be not thus,' such possibilities would also exist. But, inasmuch as this body is soulless, it is subject to suffering, and no possibility exists for (ordering): 'Let this be so, let this not be so.'

"In this same manner feelings (*vedanā*), perceptions (*saññā*), mental formations (*saṅkhāra*) and consciousness (*viññaṇa*) are soulless.

"What think ye, O bhikkhus, is this body permanent or impermanent?" "Impermanent, Ven. Sir."

"Is that which is impermanent happy or painful (*dukkha*)?" "It is painful, Ven. Sir."

"Is it justifiable then, to think of that which is impermanent, painful and transitory as: 'This is mine; this I am; this is my soul?'

"Certainly not Ven. Sir."

"Similarly, O bhikkhus, feelings, perceptions, mental formations and consciousness are impermanent and painful.

"Is it justifiable to think of these which are impermanent, painful and transitory as: 'This is mine; this I am; this is my permanent 'I'?

"Certainly not, Ven. Sir."

"Then, O bhikkhus, body, whether past, present or future, personal or external, coarse or subtle, low or high, far or near, should be understood by right knowledge in its real nature—'This is not mine (*n'etam mama*); this I am not; (*n'eso h'amasmi*); this is not my soul (*na me so attā*).'

"All feelings, perceptions, mental formations and consciousness, whether past, present or future, personal or external, coarse or subtle, low or high, far or near, should be understood by right knowledge in their real nature as: 'These are not mine: these are not I: these are not my soul.'

"The learned Ariyan disciple who sees thus gets disenchanted with body, feelings, perceptions, mental formations, consciousness, and is detached from the abhorrent thing and is emancipated through detachment. Then dawns on him the knowledge — 'Emancipated am I'. He understands that rebirth is ended, lived is the holy life, done what should be done, there is no more of this state again."

"Thus the Exalted One said, and the delighted bhikkhus applauded the words of the Exalted One."

When the Buddha expounded this teaching the minds of the group of five bhikkhus became freed of defilements without attachment.*

Discussion

The Buddha explains to the original five bhikkhus (*pañca-vaggiyas*) his doctrine of non-self or absence of a permanent and continuing 'I'. He uses a form of logic which was popular at that time called *reductio-ad-absurdum* or "reduction-to-absurdity". It is a method of counter-argument.

There are three meanings to it:

1. Proof of falsity by showing absurd logical consequences.
2. Proof of truth by thus proving falsity of alternatives.
3. Carrying of the principle to unpractical lengths.

---

* They all attained arahantship.

The fact that the *pañcavaggiyas* understood these arguments and attained arahantship is clear proof of the efficacy of the method. When we reflect on this sutta with insight and wisdom (*paññā*), we too should be able to comprehend what the Buddha had to say on the subject of *anatta*.

The Anāthapiṇḍikovada Sutta (M.143)*

There is another important sutta which we can utilize for the development of insight into the characteristic of *anatta* during intensive meditation. This is the Anāthapiṇḍikovāda Sutta.

Anāthapiṇḍika was a great benefactor of the Buddha and of the *ariya saṅgha.* When he was on his deathbed, Ven. Sāriputta and Ven. Ānanda visited him. Ven. Sāriputta had then instructed Anāthapiṇḍika as follows:

> 1. "Wherefore you, householder, must train yourself thus: 'I will not cling to the eye, and there will be no consciousness associated with the eye.' Thus should you train yourself.
> 'I will not cling to the ear ...
> 'I will not cling to the nose ...
> 'I will not cling to the tongue ...
> 'I will not cling to the body ...
> 'I will not cling to the mind ...
> Thus you should train yourself".
>
> 2. "Householder, you should train yourself thus: 'I will not cling to visual consciousness and there will be in me no consciousness associated with forms. Thus you should train yourself.
> 'I will not cling to auditory ... sounds ...

---

* (Translated by Ven M. Seelawimala Maha Thera)

'I will not cling to olfactory … smells …
'I will not cling to gustatory … tastes …
'I will not cling to tactile … tangibles …
'I will not cling to mental … thoughts …
Thus you should train yourself'.

3. "Householder, you should train yourself thus: 'I will not cling to eye-consciousness, and there will be no consciousness in me associated with eye--consciousness. Thus you should train yourself'.
'I will not cling to ear …
'I will not cling to nose …
'I will not cling to tongue …
'I will not cling to body …
'I will not cling to mind …
Thus you should train yourself'.

4. "Householder, you should train yourself thus:
'I will not cling to eye-contact and there will be no consciousness in me associated with eye-contact. Thus you should train yourself'.
'I will not cling to ear-contact …
'I will not cling to nose-contact …
'I will not cling to tongue-contact …
'I will not cling to body-contact …
Thus you should train yourself'.

5. "Householder, you should train yourself thus: 'I will not cling to sensations born of eye-contact, and will also have no consciousness born from and in association with feeling born of eye-contact. Thus you should train yourself.
'I will not cling to feeling born of ear-contact …
'I will not cling to feeling born of nose-contact, …
'I will not cling to feeling born of tongue-contact …
'I will not cling to feeling born of body-contact …
'I will not cling to feeling born of mind-contact …
Thus you should train yourself'.

6. "Householder, you should train yourself thus:
'I will not cling to the earth-element, and there will be in me no consciousness associated with the earth-element. Thus you should train yourself".
I will not cling to the water element …
I will not cling to the fire-element …
I will not cling to the air-element …
I will not cling to the space-element …
I will not cling to the consciousness element …
Thus should you train yourself".

7. "Householder, you should train yourself thus: 'I will not cling to material form and there will be in me no consciousness in association with material form. Thus you should train yourself".
I will not cling to feeling …
I will not cling to perception …
I will not cling to formations …
I will not cling to consciousness …
Thus should you train yourself".

8. "Householder, you should train yourself thus:
'I will not cling to the sphere of infinite space, and there will be in me no consciousness associated with the sphere of infinite space. Thus you should train yourself".
'I will not cling to the sphere of infinite consciousness …
'I will not cling to the sphere of nothingness …
'I will not cling to the sphere of neither-perception-nor-non-perception …
Thus should you train yourself".

(These refer to the four formless or immaterial absorptions –*jhānas*– namely: *ākāsānañcāyatana*, *viññāṇañcāyatana, ākiñ-caññāyatana* and *nevasaññā-nāsaññāyatana* respectively).

9. "Householder you should train yourself thus: 'I will not cling to this world, and there will be in me no consciousness associated with this world.
I will not cling to the world beyond, and there will be in me no consciousness associated with the world beyond'.
Thus you should train yourself".

10. "Householder, you should train yourself thus: 'I will not cling to what is heard, sensed, cognized, encountered, sought after and examined by the mind, and there will be in me no consciousness associated with that'. Thus you should train yourself."

Discussion

Anāthapiṇḍika was already a *sotāpanna* and therefore understood the true meaning contained in this advice. But for us to truly comprehend this advice it is necessary for us to first remind ourselves of how the aggregates comprising the mind work.

This is explained in the Honeyball or Madhupiṇḍika Sutta (M.18) in which the Buddha states:

"Dependent on the eye and forms, eye-consciousness arises. The meeting of the three is contact (*phassa*). With contact as condition there is feeling (*vedanā*). What one feels, that one perceives. What one perceives, that one thinks about. What one thinks about, that one proliferates. With what one has proliferated as the source, perceptions and notions tinged by mental proliferation beset a man with respect to past, future and present forms cognizable through the eye.

"Dependent on the ear, sounds... Dependent on the nose and odours... Dependent on the tongue and flavours... Dependent on the body and tangibles... Dependent on the mind and mind-objects, mind consciousness arises. The meeting of the three is contact. With contact as a condition there is feeling. What one feels, that one perceives. What one perceives, that one mentally proliferates. With what one has proliferated as the source, perceptions and notions tinged by mental proliferation beset a man with respect to the past, future and present mind-objects cognizable through the mind.

"When there is the eye, a form and eye-consciousness, it is possible to point out the manifestation of contact. When there is the manifestation of contact it is possible to point out the manifestation of feeling. When there is the manifestation of feeling, it is possible to point out the manifestation of perception. When there is the manifestation of perception, it is possible to point out the manifestation of thinking. When there is the manifestation of thinking, it is possible to point out the manifestation of being beset by perceptions and notions tinged by mental proliferation.

"When there is no eye, no form, no eye-consciousness, it is impossible to point out the manifestation of contact. When there is no manifestation of contact, it is impossible to point out the manifestation of feeling. "When there is no manifestation of thinking, it is im-possible to point out the manifestation of being beset by perceptions and notions tinged by mental proliferation."

We can visualize and then comprehend the working of the mind by looking at its primary components of contact, sensations, perception, volition and consciousness diagrammatically, along with the mental proliferations and conceiving referred to in the above sutta:

phassa (contact)
↓
vedanā (sensations)
↓
saññā (perception)
↓
vitakka, papañca (conceiving, differentiation, thinking and conceptual proliferation)
↓
saṅkhāra (volition)
↓
viññāṇa (consciousness)

Keeping the above visualization in front of us, we can now examine with *paññā* the advice given to Anāthapiṇḍika.

In the first five stanzas of the sutta, reference is to the aggregates of the body and the aggregates of mind – *rūpa* and *nāma.*

In the sixth stanza the body (*rūpa*) aggregate is further reduced to its component parts and the concept of space and consciousness are added thereto.

In the seventh stanza, Anāthapiṇḍika was advised to give up clinging to the body and to the aggregates comprising the mind (*rūpa-nāma*).

And in the eighth stanza, householders are advised to focus with non-attachment on the consciousness pertaining to the four immaterial (formless) spheres.

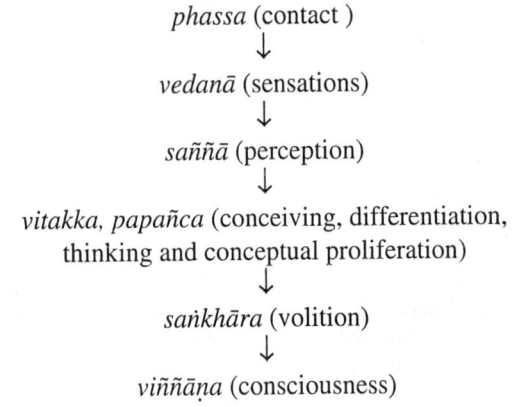

In the ninth stanza, householders are told that by this time a meditator should have achieved sufficient progress enabling him to be devoid of all clinging, and consequently there will be no clinging in a next world as well.

The householder is told that if he were to follow the advice mentioned in this final stanza, he will achieve what was stated in the previous stanza, which is **transcendence.**

Discussion

When we look at the suttas in the Majjhima Nikāya, we see that Sāriputta's above advice was in fact a more detailed description of what the Buddha had said in the Mahā Saḷāyatanika Sutta (M.149).

> "Knowing and seeing the eye, monks, as it really is, knowing and seeing forms as they really are, knowing and seeing eye-consciousness as it really is, knowing and seeing eye-contact as it really is, and knowing and seeing whatever feeling—pleasant, unpleasant or neither-pleasant-nor-unpleasant—arises dependent on eye-contact as it really is, one gets not attached to the eye, gets not attached to forms, gets not attached to eye-consciousness, gets not attached to eye-contact and gets not attached even to that feeling that arises dependent on eye-contact.
>
> "And for him as he abides unattached, unfettered, not infatuated, contemplating the peril (in the eye, ear etc.), the five aggregates of grasping go on to future diminution. That craving which makes for re-becoming decreases in him".

We should now be able to see with insight that all actions of this body-mind complex are tainted by the delusion that there is what we call a person or 'I'. But at the ultimate level there is in fact no real 'I'. We have the wrong concept of 'I". Nevertheless, we think, speak and act always influenced by this characteristic. *Vipassanā* meditation on the Anathapiṇḍikovāda Sutta makes us comprehend with insight leading to *paññā* the ultimate truth of ***anatta.*** This in turn can serve as the gateway to Nibbāna for those who are intellectually inclined.

Other dedicated meditators may perhaps find it necessary to combine the knowledge of the above with the comprehension of the Anattalakkhaṇa Sutta (Khanda Samy. 59) and/or *Paṭicca-samuppāda* (explained in the previous volume) before they can come to the very threshold of Nibbāna or to the first glimpse of Nibbāna by the attainment of the first of the four *Ariya* states, namely *sotāpanna,* and thereafter progress through the next three stages, ending with arahantship.

The Bāhiya Sutta (Ud.1.100)

The full text of the Buddha's advice to Bāhiya Dārucīriya reads as follows:

"Herein, Bāhiya, you should train yourself thus:
'In the seen will be merely what is seen;
In the heard will be merely what is heard;
In the sensed will be merely what is sensed;
In the cognized will be merely what is cognized.'
In this way you should train yourself, Bāhiya.

"When, Bāhiya, in the seen is merely what is seen;
in the heard is merely what is heard,
in the sensed is merely what is sensed,
in the cognized is merely what is cognized,

then, Bāhiya, you will not be 'with that';
when Bāhiya, you are not 'with that';
then, Bāhiya, you will not be 'in that';
when Bāhiya, you are not 'in that';
then, Bāhiya, you will be neither here nor beyond
nor in between the two,
just this is the end of suffering."

The commentaries explain these cryptic statements in the following manner:

"In the seen is merely what is seen" — see without adding one's own views, mental proliferations such as opinions and concepts, personal likes and dislikes etc. In other words, it is just seeing what is there, as it actually is.

"You will not be with that," — you will not be bound by that view, by attraction or repulsion etc.

"You will not be in that," — you will not be in a situation of being deluded and led astray by views and emotions.

"You will be neither here nor beyond nor in between the two" — then you will neither be in this world nor in another world. This would mean the experience of transcendence, Nibbāna or enlightenment, which in effect is the stepping out of the mundane world.

Discussion

So what Bāhiya comprehended with insight was the fact that "seeing, hearing, smelling" and so on are mere conditioned phenomena, and that there was no permanent "I" behind them. He thus saw the Truth, becoming thereby a liberated *Ariya*.

In the above instructions, the Buddha tells us that the concept of a permanent 'I' should be abandoned. Instead, to see with insight *anatta:* for, if there is no permanent entity called an 'I', then there is nothing to crave for or cling to. And once we abandon craving and clinging, we have broken the vicious *saṃsāric* cycle of existence: *Taṇhānirodhā upādāna-nirodho: upadāna-nirodhā bhava-nirodho: bhava-nirodhā jāti-nirodho.*

(Through the abandoning of craving 'clinging' ceases. Through the abandoning of clinging 'becoming' ceases. Through the abandoning of becoming 'rebirth' ceases).

These are the links 9, 10 and 11 of *Paṭiccasamuppāda.*

Readers would perhaps have realized that the instructions given in the sutta discussed earlier to Anātapiṇḍika were in essence similar to the brief but complete advice given to the spiritually advanced Bāhiya.

As an additional bonus we can also bring to mind the Buddha's discovery of the critically important role played by craving in the perpetuation of *saṃsāric* existence, on the night of his enlightenment, when he joyously proclaimed:

> "Through many a birth in existence wandered I
> Seeking, but not finding, the builder of this house,
> Sorrowful is repeated birth:
>
> O house-builder, thou art seen.
> Thou shalt build no house again:
> All thy rafters are broken:
> thy ridgepole is shattered:

Mind has attained to the unconditioned:
achieved is the end of cravings."*

Dhp. 153 –154
Trans. by Narada Mahathera

Concluding Remarks

The way to **awakening** is through insight wisdom into one or more of the three characteristics of the human condition, namely, impermanence, distress and absence of a permanent non-changing self or 'I' — *anicca, dukkha* and *anatta* respectively.

At the risk of repetition, it is necessary to emphasize that true comprehension and understanding of *Paṭiccasamuppāda* have the advantage that they will lead to an understanding of all of the above three characteristics of existence. For craving, clinging and birth (*vedanā, upādāna, jāti*) are phenomena that are in a constant state of flux. They are born, exist for a while (a fraction of a micro-second) and then die. This constant change is *anicca* (impermanence). Birth, decay and death — *jāti, jarā, maraṇa*— links 11 and 12, show us the inevitableness of suffering or unsatisfactoriness - *dukkha*. Finally, consciousness, name-and-form – *viññāṇa, nāma-rūpa-*, links 2 and 3, reveal *anatta*, that there is no permanent "I" or a self.

---

* House builder: craving (taṇhā); house: physical body; rafters: defilements (*kilesa*); ridgepole: ignorance; unconditioned: Nibbāna.

The Cūla Rāhulovāda Sutta (M.147)

This is another sutta in which the Buddha uses once again the technique of question and answer to instil into the mind of the recipient his teachings. The relevant part of this sutta reads as follows:

> "What do you think, Rāhula, is the eye permanent or impermanent?"
>
> "Impermanent, Ven. Sir".
>
> "Is that which is impermanent, painful or pleasant?"
>
> "It is painful, Ven. Sir".
>
> "Is it justifiable, then, to think of that which is impermanent, pain-laden and subject to change as 'This is mine; this I am; this is my self?'"
>
> "Certainly not, Ven. Sir".
>
> "What do you think Rāhula, are forms (visual objects) permanent or impermanent?"
>
> "Impermanent, Ven. Sir".
>
> "Is that which is impermanent, painful or pleasant?"
>
> "It is painful, Ven. Sir".
>
> "Is it justifiable, then, to think, of that which is impermanent, pain-laden and subject to change as 'This is mine; this I am; this is my self?'".*

"Certainly not, Ven. Sir".

"What do you think, Rāhula, is eye-consciousness (visual contact) permanent or impermanent?"

"Impermanent, Ven. Sir".

"Is that which is impermanent, painful or pleasant?'

"It is painful, Ven. Sir".

"Is it justifiable, then to think of that which is impermanent, pain-laden and subject to change as 'This is mine; this is my self?'"

"Certainly not, Ven. Sir".

"What do you think, Rāhula, that which arises conditioned by visual contact, namely all that belongs to feeling, perception, mental formations and consciousness, is that permanent or impermanent?"

"Impermanent, Ven. Sir".

"Is that which is impermanent, painful or pleasant?"

"It is painful, Ven. Sir".

"Is it justifiable, then to think of that which is impermanent, pain-laden and subject to change as 'This is mine, this I am, this is my self?'".

---

* 'This is mine' — as motivated by craving (*taṇhā*)
'This I am' — as motivated by pride (*māna*)
'This is myself' — as motivated by wrong views (*diṭṭhi*).

"Certainly not, Ven. Sir".

"What do you think, Rāhula; ear and sounds, nose and smells, tongue and tastes, body and tangibles, mind and ideas and the (corresponding types of) consciousness and contact and the feelings, perceptions, mental formations and the forms of consciousness that arise conditioned by that contact are all these permanent or impermanent?"

"Impermanent, Ven. Sir".

"Is that which is impermanent, painful or pleasant?".

"It is painful, Ven. Sir".

"Is it justifiable, then to think of that which is impermanent, painladen and subject to change as 'This is mine; this I am; this is my self?'"

"Certainly not, Ven. Sir".

"The learned noble disciple, Rāhula, who sees thus, gets disenchanted (*nibbidā*) for the eye, gets disenchanted for forms, for visual consciousness, visual contact, and for that which arises conditioned by visual contact, namely all feelings, perceptions, mental formations and forms of consciousness.

"He turns way from ear and sounds, nose and smells, tongue and tastes, body and tangibles, mind and ideas, turns away from (the corresponding types of) consciousness and contact, and from that which arises conditioned by that contact, namely all that belongs to feelings, perceptions, mental formations and consciousness".

"In him who gets disenchanted passions fade out (*virajjati*). With the fading out of passions (*virāga*) he is liberated. Thus liberated, the knowledge arises in him: 'Liberated am I, birth is exhausted, fulfilled is the holy life, done is what should be done and nothing further remains after this' Thus he knows".

Thus spoke the Blessed One. Glad at heart, venerable Rāhula rejoiced in the words of the Blessed One.

Now, during that utterance, the mind of venerable Rāhula was freed from the corruptions through clingings and there arose the stainless, immaculate Eye of Truth*: "Whatever is subject to origination is subject to cessation".

Discussion

Since this is the last of the suttas which will be discussed in this book, we can make use of this opportunity to describe a methodology which an earnest meditator could perhaps adopt in his journey towards transcendence.

The Buddha preached the Cūla Rāhulovāda Sutta (M.147) to his son Rāhula when the latter had reached twenty-one years of age. According to the commentaries, the Buddha had taken constant interest in Rāhula's development and guided him wisely through the years. There are a number of suttas addressed to Rāhula. We have looked at only the last of these suttas. One earlier to this sutta is the Mahā Rāhulovāda Sutta (M.62) which was spoken to Rāhula when he was eighteen years of age. It contains a large number of meditation subjects and, *inter-alia,* detailed instructions on *ānāpāna-sati* or mindfulness of in-and-out breathing. It appears that the Buddha considered these sub-

---

* *Dhamma-cakkhu*, the vision of Dhamma; in this case, the attainment of arahantship.

jects to be sufficient to bring Rāhula to intellectual and spiritual maturity by his twenty-first year. That this was so is proven by the fact that on hearing the Cūla Rāhulovāda Sutta (M.147), venerable Rāhula attained arahantship immediately.

This sutta contains a clear exposition of all the three characteristics of human existence, namely *anicca-dukkha-anatta,* which the advanced meditator should be able to see with application of deep and dedicated insight meditation.

A Suggested Methodology

An advanced meditator should, in the first instance, read the sutta at a normal reading speed and gather what the Buddha is telling Rāhula. Having grasped with *sutamaya-paññā* the essence of the advice, he should set the sutta aside, and recall or recollect what he already knows about the the five aggregates, which in the present context could be understood as the *pañcupādānakkhandha* or the five aggregates of clinging. He should then recollect how the aggregates become operative. Towards this end, he could conveniently refer to the topical information provided on pages 6–7, 28–29 and page 31 in the present text.

He should contemplate what he has read and develop *bhāvanāmaya-paññā.* Now, keeping the above information mentally in front of him, the advanced meditator should read the Rāhulovāda Sutta slowly and carefully, a paragraph at a time, comprehending its contents with deep insight. Next, he will review the contents of the sutta from this new perspective. On doing so, there is the possibility that he will be successful in transforming these doctrinal truths into a tangible personal experience, leading him, if all other dependent conditions at this moment are just right, to transcendence.

While a fortunate few may, in this manner, be successful at their first attempt, it may, in most cases, require repeated application. Other advanced meditators may, perhaps need similar application to some other suttas of their choice,or other methodology for fruition of their efforts. For, as we all very well know, "there are many paths leading to the top of a mountain". Finally, as I said before, our efforts should be aimed at insight knowledge of the riddle of life, rather than transcendence itself. For the latter comes automatically with the realization of the former.

CHAPTER XII

Meditating our Way to Transcendence

A significant matter that many Western *vipassanā* meditators have raised is the unavailability of simple texts that could guide meditators to insight knowledge. They have asked for a model comprising progressive but simple step-by-step meditation instructions leading to transcendence.

However, planning a programme of *vipassanā* meditation leading to transcendence is a difficult thing to do. For we can recollect that when the Buddha attempted to teach his five original disciples (the *pañcavaggiyas*), who already knew a considerable number of meditation techniques, he realized that they could not fully comprehend his first sermon, the Dhammacakkappavattana Sutta (Sacca Saṃy. 11), in the absence of insight-wisdom or *bhāvanāmaya-paññā*. The Buddha first taught them the doctrine (Dhamma) and re-moulded their way of thinking. It was only when he knew that they were in a proper frame of mind, an open mind that could understand and absorb his Dhamma, that he expounded the Anattalakkhaṇa Sutta (Khanda Samy. 59) (see Part 1, chapter 4). On listening to this sermon, all the five disciples attained arahantship.

Instead of providing us with just twenty five to fifty suttas of doctrinal discussions, the Buddha chose to preach thousands of suttas throughout his life, all encompassing one theme: suffering and the way out of suffering. We must realize that our priority is to know and understand the basics of Buddhism as contained in *Paṭiccasamuppāda*, the Four Noble Truths, *Satipaṭṭhāna* (fourfold foundation of mindfulness), *kamma* and rebirth, the manner in which the mind works as explained in the Madhupiṇḍika Sutta (M.18), the three negative behavioural patterns of the human condition (greed, hatred and delusion), and the three characteristics of human existence (impermanence, distress and the absence of an enduring ego or self or 'I'), before embarking on a voyage of discovery along the *vipassanā* path leading to transcendence.

The Buddha explicated the Dhamma to his monks in various ways, and it was left to each monk to interpret and comprehend the universal message according to his ability. Hence, by listening regularly to the Dhamma, they had the opportunity of one day hearing a sutta that struck a resonant chord in their consciousness, which in turn would triggered them to apply themselves to intensive *vipassanā* meditation leading to transcendence. This is evident from the reported instances when the Buddha found the subjects on which monks were meditating to be inappropriate, and therefore changed the subjects to the advantage of the meditators (Dhp. 25 and 285).

It is now left to us to study and meditate on the Dhamma until we come across a sutta, or even a passage from a sutta, to which we can relate, and then proceed onwards with wisdom (*paññā*) to the point where we can relate the subject of meditation to one of the three characteristics of the human condition, namely impermanence, distress and non-self. Fortunately for us, we now have a short list of doctrinal subjects on which we can concentrate (see the third paragraph of this chapter), as well as a number of suttas in the previous chapter, which can be focused on, followed by insight meditation, reflection and contemplation till we reach transcendence.

But we must first develop our morality until it is above reproach and then our power of mindfulness too is to be developed to a suitable level. We should also develop even more the *brahma-vihāras* (devine abidings) of loving-kindness, compassion, non-envious joy and equanimity. This level of development will make us fitting receptacles for receiving perhaps just one or two significant words of the Buddha and we may be fortunate enough for such revelation to trigger us towards a transcendental state.

Take the case of Bāhiya Dārucīriya (in the previous chapter), where just a few words were sufficient for him to reach immediate transcendence. Similarly, you will recollect that our experinced meditator in chapter 2 also had developed a feel for, and then studied, contemplated and meditated on the Bāhiya and the Anāthapiṇḍikovāda Suttas, which led him to transcendence. He saw the total picture, and it came to him like a flash of lightning, that the aggregates comprising a person are nothing but ever-changing conditioned phenomena, and that there is no real continuing entity or "I". He realized that his theoretical knowledge of *anatta* had actually transformed itself into experiential knowledge leading to transcendence.

In Part 1 of this book (Wheel: 450-452), the importance of *Paṭiccasamuppāda* in our progression towards liberation was emphasized, and its inter-relationship to the Four Noble Truths was shown only cursorily. But it is important at this stage to see this relationship more closely. In the Saṃyutta Nikāya the Buddha states:

> " ... the thought occurred to me, 'I have attained the path to awakening, i.e., from the cessation of name-and-form comes the cessation of consciousness, from the cessation of consciousness comes the cessation of name-and-form, from the cessation of name-and-form comes the cessation of the six sense media . . . Thus is the cessation of this entire mass of *dukkha*. Cessation, cessation.' Vision arose, clear knowing arose, discernment arose, knowledge arose, and illumination arose within me with regard to things never heard before.
>
> "It is just as if a man, travelling along a wilderness track, were to see an ancient path, an ancient road, travelled by people of former times. . . . In the same way I saw an ancient path, an ancient road, travelled by the rightly self-awakened ones in former times. What is this ... ancient path? Just this noble eightfold path: right view, right resolve, right speech, right action, right livelihood, right effort, right mindfulness, right concentration . . . I followed the path. Following it, I came to direct knowledge of the origination of ageing and death, direct knowledge of the cessation of ageing and death, direct knowledge of the path leading to the cessation of ageing and death. I followed the path. Following it, I came to direct knowledge of birth ... becoming ... clinging ... craving ... feeling ... contact ... the six sense media ... name-and-form ... consciousness ... direct knowledge of the origination of consciousness, direct knowledge of the cessation of consciousness, direct knowledge of the path leading to the cessation of consciousness. I followed that path.
>
> "Following it, I came to direct knowledge of suffering *(dukkha)*, direct knowledge of the origin of *dukkha*, direct knowledge of the path leading to the cessation of *dukkha*. Knowing that directly, I

revealed it to monks, nuns, male lay followers, and female lay followers …" (*S*.xii,65).

In view of the afore mentioned inter-relationship between *Paṭiccasamuppāda* and the Four Noble Truths, it is opportune to look closer at the latter, and in particular the First Noble Truth, which is distress *(dukkha),* for it will also give us insight into what drives us forward into future rebirths. The Buddha taught that suffering should be seen from three aspects: first is the discomfort of suffering, the second, the suffering of change, and third the pervasive suffering of the five aggregates (*khandas*), i.e., *dukkha-dukkhatā, vipariṇāma dukkha* and *saṅkhāra dukkha.*

The discomfort of suffering is ordinary suffering that we can feel in both body and mind. But, at a fundamental level, this suffering means that we are not our own masters. We are constantly under the influence and conditioning of other forces, from the external environment to the experiences and workings of our own minds and bodies. All these conditions are "other-powered" because all the causes and conditions that make up a particular moment are dependent on other things happening first, either in the environment or in our own body. This in effect is dependent origination.

The second aspect of suffering is dissatisfaction due to change. This is the dominant feature of existence *(Paṭiccasamuppāda*, link 10): that it is in constant flux. Things arise and perish (*uppāda-bhaṅga*)—for in the very midst of birth there is both creation and extinction.

The third aspect of suffering, pervasive suffering, has a two-fold meaning. First, it means that all beings experience suffering—that none can escape it. A second meaning is associated with the fourth aggregate, which is volition. For volition can work at a very subtle level. As the aggregate that leads to action, volition ensures that all living beings are constantly in a state of motion and arising. For this reason living beings cannot escape from the subtler form of pervasive suffering.

According to the *Dhamma*, there is another dimension of meaning to the five aggregates, namely 'grasping' *(upādāna)* — the ninth link in the chain of dependent origination. (Hence the aggregates are often called - *pañcupādānakkhandha*—'the five-aggregates-of-grasping'). Grasping arises when a sense faculty interacts with a sense object creating attachment, and, consequently, suffering. It is this grasping after sense experiences that assures the continuation of the five aggregates through life after life. Let us also remember that the objects of grasping are not just desires, but also hatred and delusion. Simply put, grasping causes suffering and in turn, suffering causes the continuation of the five aggregates through rebirths. On this basis we hold onto the negativities of greed, hatred and delusion (ignorance), which propel us into future rebirths. In summary, we could say that there is no suffering apart from the five aggregates, and that the escape from suffering lies in comprehension of this truth by insight and meditation.

Knowing the above, let us now try to set out a programme of development of wisdom (*paññā*) leading to transcendence. But first, a few words on *paññā*. In Buddhist philosophy wisdom *(paññā)* is described as an understanding of Dependent Origination, the Four Noble Truths, *kamma* and rebirth, the three universal characteristics of human existence namely, greed, hatred and delusion and the three verities of *anicca, dukkha* and *anatta.* But what it really implies is that *the attainment of wisdom is a transformation of the above doctrinal truths from mere intellectual knowledge into personal experience. In other words, we have to change our knowledge from book learning into actual and tangible living truths.*

This can be achieved through step-wise mental development as was explained in Part 1 of this book as *sutamaya-paññā, cintāmaya-paññā* and *bhāvanāmaya-paññā* – knowledge from reading and studying the Dhamma, a higher level of knowledge from reflecting and contemplating the Dhamma, and achieving insight knowledge by *vipassanā* meditation respectively.

There is the need to cultivate a positive attitude when attempting to understand the *Dhamma*. For, if a person listens or contemplates the *Dhamma* with an impure mind, a mind contaminated by defilements, in other words, bereft of *sīla*, then the teaching will be of little benefit. The correct attitude to be adopted when studying the *Dhamma* can be likened to a patient who pays careful attention to his physician's advice. Here the Buddha is the physician, the *Dhamma* is the medicine, and we are the patients. It is only by careful attention that we can progress in wisdom and move towards the realization of a true understanding of the *Dhamma* and from there to liberation.

In addition, let us take advantage of being able to see the Buddha's word in writing so that we can repeatedly read and refer to it as often as we wish, and have recordings which we can repeatedly play back so that we absorb, reflect and contemplate them.

However, as I have stated in Wheel 450-452, if we are really to gain insight, we need a paradigm shift whereby we 'live' in each and every one of the important suttas which we have selected for further development,. We also should not forget that mundane existence is also quite real, for when we cut ourselves it is painful. When we are abused we feel hurt and angered, and when we fall sick, it brings about agony and painful feelings. It is by using our body and mind that we can focus on the opposites to achieve transcendence. The use of opposites was exemplified when, to get rid of *loba, dosa* and *moha* – greed, hatred and delusion, we focused on *aloba, adosa* and *amoha* – non-greed, non-hatred and non-delusion. This is how we make the first differentiation of appreciating that this temporary abode is never permanent nor real, and this in turn leads us on to transcendence.

Instructions

In Wheel Publication 450-452 (pages 82-106), readers were provided with information and instructions on *vipassanā* meditation as a step-wise process. Thereafter, the *first two steps* were discussed in sufficient detail to obviate the necessity to repeat such instructions once again.

Nevertheless, it may be appropriate to emphasize the importance of *ānāpāna-sati* or in-out-breathing in the first two steps of *vipassanā* meditation. For, when we meditated on in-and-out breathing with mindfulness and concentration, we reduced the whole process of existence to a series of long and short breaths. The concept of "I" then gradually fell away. What remained was only the process of breathing. Then the "breather" or "I" too began to fade away. Thus the whole process of *ānāpāna-sati* reduces the process of life to a series of breaths in which no 'self' is present. With this realization the advanced meditator soon begins to experience the fading away of the concept of an enduring "I".

He then realizes that the efficacy of *ānāpāna-sati* can be achieved only by an impersonal attitude during *vipassanā* meditation. In other words, it is important to de-personalize the process of existence in one's mind. This in turn makes one's faculties exceptionally acute since one is not burdened with the thought "I am doing this," or "I am not doing this".

At this point in his mental development, the meditator should be able to begin viewing persons not as individuals but rather as mere aggregates of elements and, to develop this attitude of mind, a *vipassanā* meditator will contemplate the human body as consisting merely of the four fundamental elements of *āpo-tejo-vāyo-paṭhavi* or water, fire, air and earth.* This he does only mentally, and from there it is just one more step to the realization that all forms of existence are mere processes thereby realizing the true nature of phenomena.

What is then left is to discuss the third or final step in the *vipassanā* practice that will lead the practitioner to transcendence. We should, perhaps, also understand that in addition to

---

* See note 11 of chapter IX.

the *vipassanā* meditation practice, a type of consciousness or mental event called the 'supramundane path' achieves the breakthrough to the Unconditioned. This occurs in four stages, and each in turn is also called a "path".

These four supramundane paths have the special task of eradicating certain defilements, the fetters *(saṃyojana)*. These defilements are not strangers to the meditator, for they bothered him in the previous stages of concentration and preliminary insight meditation where these defilements were not totally eradicated. They were only checked and suppressed, and deep beneath the surface they continued to linger as latent negative tendencies as *anusaya*. But, when the supramundane paths are reached, the real work of eradication begins.

These defilements act as fetters or shackles (*saṃyojana*) and are ten in number:

1. Illusion of a continuing 'self', *(sakkāya-diṭṭhi)*
2. Doubts *(vicikicchā)*
3. Adherence to rites and ceremonies *(sīlabbata-parāmāsa)*
4. See desires *(kāma-rāga)*
5. Ill will *(paṭigha)*
6. Attachment to the sphere of forms *(rūparāga)*
7. Attachment to the formless-sphere *(arūpa-rāga)*
8. Conceit *(māna)*
9. Restlessness *(uddhacca)*
10. Ignorance *(avijjā)*.

When the advanced *vipassanā* meditator begins realizing Nibbāna for the first time, he is called a *sotāpanna* – One who has entered the Path or stream that leads to Nibbāna. He is no more a worldling, but an *Ariya* – a Noble One. He eliminates the three fetters of self-illusion (*sakkāya diṭṭhi*), doubts (*vicikicchā*), and adherence to wrongful rites and ceremonies (*sīlabbata parāmāsa*). As he has not eliminated all the fetters, he is reborn a maximum of seven times. In his subsequent birth he may or may not be aware of the fact that he is a *sotāpanna*. Nevertheless, he possesses the characteristics of an *Ariya*. He is moreover absolved from birth in states of woe since he is destined for enlightenment.

Stimulated by this first glimpse of Nibbāna, the *Ariya* pilgrim can now make rapid progress, and perfecting his insight he becomes a *sakadāgāmin* or once-returner by attenuating two other fetters, namely sense-desire *(kāma-rāga*) and ill-will (*paṭigha*). A *sakadāgāmin* is reborn on earth only once. It is interesting to note that a *sakadāgāmin* can only weaken these two fetters, and may infrequently be bothered by thoughts of sensuality and repugnance to a slight extent, which he then consciously suppresses.

It is by attaining the third stage of saint-hood called *anāgāmin* (non-returner) that he completely eliminates the above two fetters of *kāma-rāga* and *paṭigha*. Thereafter he neither returns to this world nor to a celestial realm, for he is reborn in the 'Pure Abodes" reserved for them from where they attain Nibbāna.

The *anāgāmin*, encouraged by the success of his efforts now makes his final advance and, destroying the remaining five fetters of attachment to the form-spheres (*rūpa-rāga*), attachment to formless-spheres (*arūpa-rāga*), conceit (*māna*), restlessness (*uddhacca*), and ignorance (*avijjā*), attain *arahantship*, the final stage of sainthood.

Step Three in the *Vipassanā* Practice

This is the final and most important stage of *vipassanā* meditation. It is to follow the Buddha's instructions of bare and simple observation of everything happening in this body, avoiding proliferation of thoughts, with a mind free of concepts and orientated to simply seeing and then letting go. Therefore, from now onwards we would not need any more doctrinal material, for we already have instilled into our minds sufficient *dhamma* from the suttas enumerated in chapter XI.

As experienced *vipassanā* meditators, we can also consider ourselves as persons who have started to practise the Noble Eightfold Path and that we have developed the *brahma-vihāras* to a reasonable extent. Consequently, our minds have begun to acquire a certain amount of spiritual tranquillity. We are also firm observers of the five precepts at all times and in some cases the eight precepts. These bring about contentment. We have also trained ourselves to be restrained in regard to the five mental hindrances (*nīvaraṇa*) of:

kāmacchanda (lust),
vyāpāda (ill-will),
thīnamiddha (sloth and torpor),
uddhaccakukkucca (restlessness and anxiety) and
vicikicchā (doubt).

We can now, according to the Mūlapariyāya Sutta (M.1), consider ourselves as *noble worldlings,* (i.e., worldlings practising the course of training in insight meditation leading to the attainment of a supramundane path).

Being now mindful of all bodily functions, we become conscious only of a whole series of actions taking place. We do not in any way think of these actions as being performed by an "I". In this fashion, activities such as walking, sitting, observing, thinking begin to be recognized as only a series of impersonal actions. With this kind of mind training, one's faculties become exceptionally 'fine-tuned', since one is not burdened with the thought that "I am doing this, or I am not doing this".

It is now quite easy to develop concentration supported by scrupulous morality and dedication to a desire to understand impermanence, suffering and absence of a permanent "I" *at the experiential level.* We leave all concepts aside and focus on the five aggregates comprising body and mind. It is a paradigm shift involving our total immersion in *Paṭiccasamuppāda*, the Four Noble Truths as well as the four Foundations of Mindfulness (the four *satipaṭṭhānas*).

We do not try to achieve anything. We do not use a checklist to measure our progress against it. We simply observe everything occurring in body and mind with equanimity. Doing so also contributes to our inner purification, for we are continuously developing non-greed, non-hatred and freedom from the delusion of a permanent self. As we advance in meditation, we shall see before our very eyes the appearance, existence and the passing away of all phenomena (*uppāda, ṭhithi, bhaṅga*). The resulting disenchantment leads to still more determination, and we continue insight meditation with equanimity.

Whoever has not penetrated the impersonality of all existence, and does not comprehend that in reality there exists only a continuously self-consuming process of arising and passing away of bodily and mental phenomena, and that there is no ego-entity within or outside this process, will not be able to understand the Truth. For he will think that it is his ego, his personality, which experiences the suffering, his personality that performs good and evil actions and will be reborn according to *kamma.* He also thinks that his personality will enter into Nibbāna, and that it is his personality that walks on the Noble Eightfold Path!

This is the point at which the meditator should once again revert to contemplating *Paṭiccasamuppāda* in the forward (*anuloma*) as well as the reverse direction (*paṭiloma*) with mindfulness and constant awareness (*sati-sampajañña)* of impermanence and non-self. Or in the alternative, like the experinced meditator of chapter IX, he can focus, contemplate and reflect on the inner truths contained in one or more of the suttas discussed in the previous chapter, by deep insight meditation.

It will then be just a matter of time before he realizes the truth of either anicca *or* dukkha *or* anatta *experientially.*

Let us summarize what we have been saying so far. We started by looking at the Dhamma in books, followed by intensive reflection on the teachings, which in turn led to an intellectual understanding of the Dhamma. But it was when we used the mind to contemplate the body that true wisdom arose. When there is wisdom in our minds, then, wherever we look, there is the Dhamma and we see *anicca, dukkha* and *anatta* at all times.

The Buddha has shown us that there is no higher practice than to see that 'this is not my self and this does not belong to me', and that 'me' and 'mine' are simply conventional terms. When we understand everything clearly in this way, we will be at peace. When we realize in the present moment the truth of impermanence, that things are not ourselves or do not belong to us, then, when things disintegrate, we are at peace with them, because they do not belong to anybody, anyway. They are merely the elements of earth, water, wind and fire. *

Let me conclude this critically important chapter with a few excerpts from the teachings of Achan Chah, who was one of the foremost meditation masters of the twentieth century and who has been regarded as a monk who had attained the bliss of Nibbāna.[1]

> "There is a fundamental difference between studying the Dhamma and applying it in the practice, for true Dhamma has only one purpose—to show a way out of the distress—*dukkha* in our lives. Our suffering has causes for its arising and a place to abide. Therefore the Buddha taught us to contemplate the movements of the mind. Watching the mind move, we can see its basic characteristics—endless change, distress and emptiness. This, in fact, is the process of Dependent Origination.

---

* See note 11 of chapter IX.

"The Buddha taught us to let go, and just let them be— both the good and the bad. But for us to know how it is possible to give them up, it is necessary to study and observe our minds. This we can do only through meditation, for the only true knowledge is to see what is within ourselves. Therefore, when we develop *samādhi* and *vipassanā* — concentration and insight, and these arise in the mind, we have to use them fruitfully. Otherwise one will know only the words of Buddhism.

"Dhamma is everywhere you look. There is nothing in the world that is not Dhamma. But you must understand that happiness and unhappiness, pleasure and pain, in fact *the vicissitudes of life or worldly dhammas*[2] *are always with us. When you understand their nature, the Buddha and the Dhamma are right there.* It is simple and direct once you understand. When pleasant things arise, understand them as empty. When unpleasant things arise, understand that they are not you or yours, for they pass away. If you do not relate to phenomena as being you or see yourself as their owner, the mind comes into balance. This balance is the correct path, the correct teaching of the Buddha that leads to liberation, to non-grasping, to *vimutti*.

The Buddha only sees you to the beginning of the Path: *akkhātāro tathāgatā*—the Tathāgatas only point the way. It's up to you now".

—Ajahn Chah

Let us ponder what this illustrious teacher had to s
now have the wisdom and the dedication to break th
comprehend with *bhāvanāmaya paññā*, the chara
anicca, dukkha or *anatta*. There will also come th
can achieve transcendence in the same manner
and our experinced meditator has done. But o
yet complete for, at best, we have only att
Ariya paths. We are 'learners' and have
three of the fetters *(saṃyojana)* that

way we need to proceed thereafter is discussed in the final chapter.

CHAPTER XIII

Concluding Remarks

We are all fellow-travellers in *saṃsāra*. How we entered this maze, this labyrinth, is beyond human perception. We are constantly subject to suffering, although most of the time we conceive this suffering as pleasure, because very often suffering is sugarcoated. We also have a tendency to think that any pain we experience is something we can live with by accepting the adage that "there is no pleasure without pain". This is as much an illusion as it is to scratch oneself intensively when we itch, or as in the unfortunate case of lepers who try to deaden the pain in their extremities by holding them to a flame as the lesser of the two evils. It is only when suffering is catastrophic that we sit up and take notice.

To end suffering we need to understand the fundamental cause of suffering, which is ignorance. But this truth has to be understood not intellectually but as a direct experience and this is possible only with intensive *vipassanā* meditation. We also need to recognize the difference between understanding *Paṭiccasamuppāda, Satipaṭṭhāna* and the Four Noble Truths intellectually, and seeing them directly.

The key to this understanding is to recognize that what we see are only phenomena and that all phenomena are empty of an enduring self. This in turn leads to the understanding of **emptiness** (*suññatā*) of all *dhammas* or phenomena.

With the proper understanding of the three characteristics of human existence as impermanent, unsatisfactory and empty of 'self', these delusions are removed and wisdom arises, and with this wisdom we can penetrate and experience liberation — Nibbāna.

The Buddha, in the Mūlapariyāya Sutta (M.1), has shown that human-kind could be divided spiritually into four classes of people:

1. The ordinary worldling (i.e., one who is not practising meditation),
2. The noble worldling (i.e., a worldling practising the course of training in insight meditation with a view to attaining the supramundane path),
3. The learner (the *Ariya* who is on the Path — *sotāpanna, sakadāgāmin* and *anāgāmin*),
4. The non-learner (i.e. the *arahant*).

The ordinary worldling is destined to continue his journey in *saṃsāra* with no end in sight.

The noble worldling is a person who has kept the moral precepts, been generous, cultivated the *brahma-vihāras* and meditated with insight, but had not been able to make a breakthrough to enter the Path in this lifetime. He is now free from birth in disadvantaged *loka* (worlds), but will travel in *saṃsāra* perfecting his *pāramitās* and inclined towards Nibbāna until he is able to make a break-through to enlightenment.

The 'learner' is one who has successfully entered the Path in this very life. He is now an *Ariya* and is destined to have at a maximum only seven more rebirths either in the heavens or on earth until he achieves liberation. He has eliminated the three fetters of self-illusion, doubt and adherence to wrongful rites and ceremonies, and thus become a *sotāpanna*, but has not eradicated all the fetters that bind him to existence.

The *Ariyan* pilgrim now makes rapid progress, and by perfecting his insight, attenuates the two fetters of sense-desires and ill-will and thereby becomes a *sakadāgāmin*. A *sakadāgāmin* is reborn on earth only once, in case he has not attained arahatship in that life itself.

Now he totally eliminates the above two fetters of sense-desires and ill-will and thereby becomes an *anāgāmin*. If he fails to persevere and attain arahantship in this existence, he is destined to end his days in a *suddhāvāsa* Brahma-world that is reserved for them.

Finally, there is the worldling who is born in this world with his *pāramitās* fully developed. He will be a person with the highest of moral rectitude. He will either leave the lay-life or spend most of his time in meditation, contemplation and reflection on the Dhamma till he makes a breakthrough with wisdom and attains *Nibbana* in this very life as an *arahant*.

Once we are aware of the above hierarchy and know where we presently stand, it is possible for us then to decide what our aspirations should be. Only then can we apply ourselves accordingly in terms of morality, concentration and development of wisdom by insight (*vipassanā*) meditation. We should remember the inspiring way in which the Buddha described his Dhamma:

svākkhāto bhagavatā dhammo sandiṭṭhiko, akāliko, ehipassiko, opanayiko, paccattaṃ veditabbo viññūhi'ti.

"Well explained is the teaching of the Blessed One; of immediate benefit, timeless, inviting us to experience it, leading us onwards, and *to be comprehended individually by the wise*".

The words 'to be comprehended individually by the wise' affirm what we had previously known experientially: that it is only by developing *bhāvanāmaya paññā* or wisdom through insight-meditation that we can comprehend the Dhamma individually. Mundane truths take on a new dimension and now become supramundane truths. What was theoretical knowledge becomes experiential knowledge, and then all actions become effortless, for craving and clinging have been understood and eliminated.

But the final breakthrough to transcendence can be quite elusive, to the chagrin of many an advanced meditator. It then becomes necessary for the dedicated meditator to exercise equanimity and to look inwards with an open mind and see whether there are any defilements yet remaining within oneself and also whether one has successfully developed the seven *bojjhaṅgas* or seven factors of enlightenment, namely: mindfulness, investigation, effort, rapture, calm, concentration and equanimity (*sati, dhamma-vicaya, viriya, pīti, passaddhi, samādhi* and *upekkhā*).

It is assumed that by now these factors are developed and present in all of our advanced meditators. If, however, the serious meditator finds himself wanting in this regard, he should quickly resort to developing these factors by means of *vipassanā* meditation, for in the Ānāpānasati Sutta the Buddha states: "Bhikkhus, ... the seven enlightenment factors, developed and cultivated, fulfill true knowledge and deliverance".

It is also interesting to note that these factors of enlightenment which bring the advanced meditator to transcendence, can bring healing to sicknesses as evinced in the Bojjhaṅga (Gilāna) Suttas (Bojjhaṅga Saṃy. 14, 15, and 16).

Summary of the Final Practical Steps Leading to Transcendence

1. Achieve concentration and one-pointedness
2. Live experiencing *Paṭiccasamuppāda* and the Four Noble Truths.
3. Experience the fading away of the concept of "I" during *ānāpāna* meditation.
4. Similarly, experience *uppāda, ṭhithi* and *bhaṅga.*
5. Develop equanimity even more.
6. Experiential realization of conditionality and emptiness.

7. Letting go of all experiences in body and mind, and recognizing them as mere phenomena and formations.

By travelling together along the *vipassanā* path we have come to the threshold of Awakening. We are just a step away. Only a bit more sustained *vipassanā* meditation is now required. This is in the form of intensive insight contemplation by picturing oneself in the cycle of conditioned existence—*Paṭiccasamuppāda*, or by total immersion in one or more of the aforementioned suttas, Anāthapiṇḍikovāda, Anattalakkhaṇa (Khanda Saṃy. 59), Bāhiya (Ud.1.10) and Rāhulovāda (M.143) Suttas, or by intensive application to the meditation subjects mentioned in the Mahā Satipaṭṭhāna Sutta (D.22).

The above paragraph does not mean that the suttas which can trigger the earnest meditator to transcendence are limited to the ones mentioned in the previous paragraph. On the contrary, most of the suttas of the Buddha have this potential. But, if we are asked for a short list, we would, in addition to the above, recommend (with our limited knowledge of the suttas), the Ānāpānasati Sutta, the Girimānanda Sutta (A.X.60), the Mahā Kassapa Thera Bojjhaṅga Sutta (Bojjhaṅga Saṃy. 14)
, the Upanisā Sutta (Nidāna Saṃy. 23) and the Māluṅkyaputta Sutta (Salāyatana Saṃy. 95), as ones which, when read with *sati-sampajañña* (mindfulness and awareness), may catalyze the fruition of insight wisdom *(sutamaya-paññā)* leading to transcendence.

It is important to remember that we must strive for wisdom (*paññā*) regarding the truth of existence, namely *anicca, dukkha* and *anatta* (impermanence, distress and non-self) and not to strive for awakening or liberation.

Once we have passed through the above stages and achieved insight wisdom, enabling us to "enter the path" and thus making us *Ariyas*, there is very little more to be done. All that remains is for us to observe everything happening in this fathom-long body and then to let go. By doing so, we should be able gradually to eliminate the rest of the *saṃyojanas* (fetters) that hold us back from total liberation.

Awakening will come naturally once the mind is pure and open, when our *pāramitās* are appropriately developed and we have penetrated the cause and conditions of existence and also we have sufficient supporting conditions to realize the bliss of liberation.

We should, and only then, be able to boldly say:

"This is the **Fourfold Truth**.
It must be comprehended with wisdom.
It has been comprehended with wisdom.

"This is the **Doctrine of Dependent Origination.**
It must be comprehended with wisdom.
It has been comprehended with wisdom.

These are the ***Satipaṭṭhānas.***
They have to be meditated upon.
They have been meditated upon,
and comprehended with wisdom.

The End

Selected Reading

1. *The Seven Stages of Purification* by Ven Mahathera Sri Nanarama. BPS Publication. ISBN 955-24-0059-7.
2. *Looking Inward* By Tan Acharn Kor Khao-suan-luang. BPS Wheel, No 373/374.
3. *Directing to Self-Penetration*. BPS Wheel No. 326-328.
4. *The Seven Contemplations of Insight* By Ven. Sri Nanarama, BPS Publication, ISBN 955-24-0124-0.

Some *Vipassanā* Meditation Centres and Retreats in the U.S.A.

1. Insight Meditation Society, U.S.A. 123 Pleasant Street, Barre, MA 01005.
2. Chico Dharma Study Foundation, Director, Peter D. Santina, 26 Kirkway, Chico, CA 59289.
3. Mettā Forest Monastery, Director, Ven Thanissaro Bhikkhu, P.O.Box 1409, Valley Center, CA 92082.
4. Vippassanā Meditation Center (Goenka), P.O.Box24, Shelbourne Falls, MA 01370.
5. Bhāvanā Society, Director, Ven Henepola Gunaratana, Route 1, Box 218-3, High View, WV 26808
6. Spirit Rock Meditation Center, P.O.Box 169, Woodacre, CA 94973.

Some Vipassanā Meditation Centres and Retreats in the U.S.A.

7. Abhayagiri Buddhist Monastery, 16201, Tomki Road, Redwood Valley, CA 05470.

Notes

Chapter VIII

1. *Ariyas*: The Noble Ones. Those who are on the Path. See note 1 of chapter X.

2. *Pāramitās* or *Pāramī*: These are the ten perfections which are requisites for enlightenment. They are: *dāna* (generosity), *sīla* (morality), *nekkhamma* (renunciation), *paññā* (wisdom), *viriya* (exertion, effort), *khanti* (forbearance), *sacca* (truthfulness), *adihiṭṭhāna* (determina-tion), *mettā* (loving-kindness), and *upekkhā* (equanimity). For more details, see *A Treatise on the Pāramīs* by Acariya Dhammapala. B.P.S. Wheel Publication, 409-411.

3. See also kchapter 4 of Part 1.

Chapter IX

1. *Jhāna*: meditative absorption of the mind. The *jhānas* are achieved through the attainment of full concentration.

2. Sāti. During the time of the Buddha there was a bhikkhu called Sāti. It is best to quote the details of the incident by direct reference from the Mahātaṇhāsaṅkhaya Sutta (M.38):

   "And the Blessed One then asked him:" Sāti, is it true that he following pernicious view has arisen in you: 'As I understand the Dhamma taught by the Blessed One it is this same consciousness that runs and wanders through the round of rebirths, not another'?"

   "Yes, Ven. sir"

   "What is this consciousness, Sāti?"

"Venerable Sir, it is that which speaks and feels and experiences here and there the results of good and bad actions."

"Misguided man, to whom have you ever known me to teach the Dhamma in that way?". ... in many discourses have I not stated that consciousness to be dependently arisen, since without condition there is no origination of consciousness?... "

3. Bodhisatta: A person aspiring to be a Buddha in a future rebirth

4. *Kappa*: eon or aeon: A "world-period", is an inconceivably long period of time. "How long a world-dissolution will continue, how long the chaos, how long the formation, how long the continuation of the formed world universe? Of these things, O Monks, one hardly can say that it will be so many years, or so many centuries, or so many millennia, or so many hundreds of thousands of years." (A. VII,62).

   The beautiful simile S. XV, 5 states "Suppose, O monks, there was a huge rock of solid mass, one mile long, one mile wide and one mile high, without split or flaw and at the end of every hundred years a man should come and rub against it once with a silken cloth. Then that huge rock would wear off and disappear quicker than a world-period. But of such world-periods, O monks, many have passed away, many hundreds, many thousands, many hundreds of thousands. And how is this possible? Inconceivable, O monks, is this *saṃsāra*, not to be discovered is any first beginning of beings who, obstructed by ignorance and ensnared by craving, are hurrying and hastening through this round of rebirths." S. XV 5. (From. Nyanatiloka: *Buddhist Dictionary,* 1980, BPS.)

5. Lily de Silva; *Nibbana as a Living Experience.* Wheel Publication 407-408, BPS.

6. Brahmin: The caste regarded as the highest in India during the time of the Buddha.

7. *Vipassanā-upakkilesa.* See footnote 8 on page 51 of Sri Ñāṇārāma: *The Seven Stages of Purification and Insight Knowledges.*

8. *Saṅkhāra-upekkhā:* See *op.cit.* page 36.

9. The meaning of this verse:

> "Whosoever has not penetrated this impersonality of all existence, and does not comprehend that in reality there exists only this continually self-consuming process of arising and passing bodily and mental phenomena, and that there is no separate ego-entity within or outside this process, he will not be able to understand the *Dhamma*. For, he will think that it is his ego, his personality that experiences the suffering, his personality that performs good and evil actions and will be reborn according to these actions-his personality that will enter Nibbāna, his personality that walks on the Noble Eightfold Path etc.
>
> "Whosoever is not clear with regard to the conditionally arisen phenomena, and does not comprehend that all actions are conditioned by ignorance etc., he thinks that it is an ego that understands or does not understand, that acts or causes to act, that comes to existence at rebirth — that has the sense impressions, that feels, desires, becomes attached, continues and at rebirth again enters a new existence" *(Vis.XVI).*

10. See Srī Ñāṇārāma note [7] above.

11. The four elements (*dhatu*) consist of *apo* (water), *tejo* (fire), *vāyo* (wind), and *paṭhavi* (earth), which correspond to the physical qualities of cohesion, caloricity, motion and solidity resptectively.

Chapter X

1. The four and eight described are the four types of *Ariyas* or the Noble Ones — *sotāpanna, sakadāgāmi, anāgāmi* and *arahat*. First they arrive at the respective four *ariya* paths (*magga*), and then enjoy the fruits of such achievement. Hence four become eight (*phala*).

2. *A Flash of Lightning in the Dark of the Night.* Dalai Lama, 1994, ISBN 0-87773-971-4.

Chapter XII

1. *The Living Dhamma* by Ven Ajahn Chah. Reprinted and distributed by The Corporate Body of the Buddha Educational Foundation, Taiwan, 1995.

2. Worldly dhammas or the vicissitudes of life: they are the worldly conditions of gain and loss, fame and defame, praise and blame, and happiness and pain.

About the Author

Ron Wijewantha was born in Sri Lanka in 1925. He received his BSc (Hon.) degree from the University of Ceylon in 1949, and thereafter the BSC (Hon.) degree and the MSc degrees from the London University. The University of California awarded him the PhD degree in 1963. He now lives in retirement in California after a long and distinguished career in Sri Lanka's State Services.

Dr Wijewantha is a devout Buddhist and was ordained a member of the Sangha for a short period. He now spends most of his time in study of the Dhamma and in practising *vipassanā* meditation. He is also a reputed *vipasanā* instructor and author of *The Life and Message of the Buddha* (A book for Young People) and ~~*Paṭiccasamuppāda*~~*Paṭiccasamuppāda (Dependent origination)* — *The Road to Liberation* (Wheel Publication 450-452).

About this Book

This book is a sequel to Ron Wijewantha's presentation on *Paṭiccasamuppāda* as the *Road to Liberation*. (B.P.S. Wheel Publication 450-452). In the present volume, the author elaborates on the doctrinal knowledge and meditation methodology which are a *sine-qua-non* for current *vipassanā* meditators at an advanced stage of progress to adopt, if they are to make a breakthrough to transcendence. For, as he points out, many an advanced meditator has to his chagrin found that Transcendence is extremely difficult to attain without ~~with~~ proper guidance.